A GUIDE TO WORSHIP MINISTRY

A GUIDE TO WORSHIP MINISTRY

The Worship Minister's Life and Work

Gregory B. Brewton

WIPF & STOCK · Eugene, Oregon

A GUIDE TO WORSHIP MINISTRY
The Worship Minister's Life and Work

Copyright © 2018 Gregory B. Brewton. All rights reserved. Except for brief quotations in critical publications or reviews, no part of this book may be reproduced in any manner without prior written permission from the publisher. Write: Permissions, Wipf and Stock Publishers, 199 W. 8th Ave., Suite 3, Eugene, OR 97401.

Wipf & Stock
An Imprint of Wipf and Stock Publishers
199 W. 8th Ave., Suite 3
Eugene, OR 97401

www.wipfandstock.com

PAPERBACK ISBN: 978-1-4982-9693-9
HARDCOVER ISBN: 978-1-4982-9695-3
EBOOK ISBN: 978-1-4982-9694-6

Manufactured in the U.S.A.   01/17/18

Scripture quotations are from the ESV® Bible (The Holy Bible, English Standard Version®), copyright © 2001 by Crossway, a publishing ministry of Good News Publishers. Used by permission. All rights reserved.

To my wife, Holly, who encouraged me all along
the way to see this project to its completion.

Contents

Introduction | ix

Section I: Considering Worship Ministry
Chapter 1: Has God Called You to Worship Ministry? | 3
Chapter 2: A Call to Worship Ministry Is a Call to Prepare | 9
Chapter 3: A Blueprint for Worship Ministry | 13
Chapter 4: Getting Started in Worship Ministry | 18

Section II: Leading the Worship Ministry
Chapter 5: Working with Your Pastor | 27
Chapter 6: The Daily Life of the Worship Leader | 31
Chapter 7: Being Above Reproach | 34
Chapter 8: Loving People | 39
Chapter 9: The Worship Minister's Family | 43
Chapter 10: Organizing Your Week—Time Management in Worship Ministry | 49
Chapter 11: Planning the Worship Ministry Calendar | 54
Chapter 12: The Worship Pastor's Resources (Budgeting) | 58
Chapter 13: Hospital Ministry | 63
Chapter 14: Dealing with Conflicts | 67

Section III: Preparing for Sunday
Chapter 15: Planning the Worship Service | 73
Chapter 16: Shaping the Order of Worship | 84
Chapter 17: Planning Worship for Special Occasions | 94

Chapter 18: Leading and Evaluating the Worship Service | 99
Chapter 19: Worship Leading for Life | 105

Section IV: Discipling through Worship Ministry
Chapter 20: Discipling Your Worship Teams | 115
Chapter 21: Discipling the Generations through Worship Ministry | 121
Chapter 22: Worship Ministry to Children | 125
Chapter 23: Worship Ministry to Students | 134
Chapter 24: The Worship Choir | 142
Chapter 25: Worship Ministry to Senior Adults | 147
Chapter 26: Safeguarding the Worship Ministry | 151
Chapter 27: When It Is Time to Move | 160
Chapter 28: Some Closing Thoughts | 165

Bibliography | 169

Introduction

> Him we proclaim, warning everyone and teaching everyone with all wisdom,
> that we may present everyone mature in Christ.
> Colossians 1:28

THE APOSTLE PAUL VIEWED discipleship as a top priority in the church—presenting everyone mature in Christ. Those shepherding the church seek to equip the saints for the work of ministry (Eph 4:12). No matter what area of local church ministry a person is called to lead, a primary task of that ministry is discipleship. Worship ministry is no different. Worship ministers make disciples through intentional worship planning and leading. They train and equip their teams weekly. They disciple small groups and mentor others one on one.

Yes, a call to worship ministry in large part is still about worship leading, but it is so much more. This book considers the many facets of worship ministry, from leading your congregation in worship each Sunday to the weekly rehearsals of your worship teams. Topics range from determining your call to ministry to working with your pastor and caring for your family, with the discipleship theme interwoven throughout the chapters.

This book has been many years in the making. Many of the principles that I share are gathered from worship leaders and pastors who have been wonderful examples to me in my formative years of worship ministry. Some of the ideas come from experiences I had over many years of church ministry—most joyful and a few difficult. I have sought to let the Bible ground the principles that I share. It is ultimately a guidebook to ministry.

The writing of this book grew out of a desire to have a resource for my worship ministry classes at The Southern Baptist Theological Seminary and

Introduction

our undergraduate school, Boyce College. I am grateful to the Lord for the opportunity he has given me to work with some of the most inspiring and encouraging worship students on the planet. I am hoping this resource is useful to the young worship leader as well as seasoned worship leaders who want to refresh their thoughts on worship ministry.

I found the writing of this guide to worship ministry challenging due to the varied way churches view worship ministry. I do not at all pretend to be the final authority on this topic, but seek to draw from my own experience serving as a worship minister. You will need to adapt these ideas and principles based on your unique church setting. The worship ministry should be contextual and all the while still grounded in biblical principles. Hopefully what is shared in these pages will encourage you as a worship minister to love your people more and help them to mature in Christ. In the final analysis worship ministry should be all about making much of Christ.

SECTION I

Considering Worship Ministry

CHAPTER 1

Has God Called You to Worship Ministry?

MY STORY (BRIEFLY)

I BEGAN MY MINISTRY journey early growing up in a Christian home. I think we were at church for almost every service and activity. Even though neither of my parents were musicians, I developed a love for music as a child. During my school years I had many musical opportunities in choirs and band programs, and gained some understanding of music reading and instrumental skills. While in high school I served in the student ministry at my church, participated in choirs and led worship in student settings. At this church I grew deeper in my walk with Christ. I sensed God calling me to ministry, but I had no idea how that looked beyond high school. Our church's music minister made a great impact on me as I considered this calling. I thought perhaps God was calling me to serve a church in the same capacity as my music minister.

As I began my freshman year in college I decided to major in music, believing that music would play a role in my future ministry. While in college I had worship leading opportunities in small church settings and college worship gatherings, which helped me see the Lord's leading in this calling. Following college I continued to pursue worship ministry training at seminary, where I completed a graduate degree in church music. After graduating from seminary I served for almost twenty years in full-time worship ministry in the church before I returned to seminary to do additional worship studies in a doctoral program.

Section I: Considering Worship Ministry

DISCERNING GOD'S CALL

How do you know if you are called to worship ministry? I wish there was a simple assessment test like the SAT or ACT that helped to determine this calling, but it is not that easy. God calls men and women into ministry, but the path he leads them to this ministry can be different from person to person. First, to clarify, all of those who know Christ as their Lord and Savior are called to serve. The Apostle Paul admonishes Christians to be "always abounding in the work of the Lord" (1 Cor 15:58). Peter tells us to use our gifts to serve one another in the church (1 Pet 4:10). Every Christian is called to serve, but some are called to do this ministry vocationally. Is God calling you into a vocational worship ministry? Here are some questions to contemplate as you attempt to discern the call to ministry.

Often times when asked about how they received the call to ministry, people respond that they "felt" a call. This may be true, but "feeling" God's call can be so subjective and sometimes hard to recognize. When people say they have a call to ministry, it is the coming together of a number of life events such as personal family background, relationships, and interests that culminate in a call to ministry. God uses these life events to direct a person towards a place of service.

A good place to start in this journey is to contemplate whether you feel a strong compulsion towards vocational ministry. Do you have a strong sense of commitment and purpose to do ministry? People may think of this call as a career choice, but it is more of a lifetime commitment and a passion to serve the Lord in his church than a career choice. Pastor John Piper wrote a book directed to those serving in ministry called *Brothers, We Are Not Professionals*. The basic premise of the book focuses on the worldly concept of ministry as a professional career. Piper says the pastoral ministry is not about having a professional career but a calling that is spiritual. The worship minister must humbly serve and shepherd Christ's church. God may lead you to a full-time vocational calling in ministry or perhaps to a bivocational or volunteer ministry position. Sometimes God calls a minister to gain employment away from the church in order to serve a church that cannot afford a full-time minister.

The calling to worship ministry is first a calling to ministry. The position of "worship" minister is not one of the ministry callings seen in the New Testament. It is not on a list of ministries seen in the Epistles nor do we see "student" ministers, "children" ministers, "discipleship" ministers, or "recreation" ministers mentioned. It is vital for worship ministers to understand that their primary calling to ministry is to shepherd and disciple the body of Christ. Worship ministry is not really about music but about people. After discerning that we are called to ministry, we then use the gifts he has given us to serve the church, such as musical abilities the Lord has given us.

Another consideration for someone who is exploring a call to worship ministry concerns gifting. A person must ask, "Has God given me the gifts necessary to do this ministry?" Occasionally, I will meet a student who desires to study worship ministry but does not appear to have the musical aptitude for such ministry. The student may have a passion for music but limited ability, musical training, or experience. I often counsel such a student to consider another ministry area since the aptitude and ability to do musical things seems limited. Middle school and high school students who hope to study music in college should get as much musical experience and training as possible in these early years. Playing in instrumental groups, seeking private musical instruction, singing in choirs, and serving in different roles in the worship ministry of the church will all help to launch a person who desires to serve in worship ministry.

In some churches today it is possible to be involved and even lead a worship ministry with no formal training in music. There are many gifted worship ministers who lack the training of a college music program. This works well for some leaders, but a call to serve in worship ministry should be a call to get musical training. Worship leaders should be able to speak the language of music to other musicians in their churches. If a worship leader wants to write and arrange worship music, formal music training is essential. For many years of fruitful worship ministry, developing all of the foundational music skills is invaluable.

Here's another way to think about preparation. Getting the musical training you need to more effectively carryout your calling is really not about you. It's about the many people you will impact over the years of ministry who will benefit from your training. When you think about it, the opportunity to train and prepare in college and seminary is a brief time compared to the many years ahead of serving in ministry. It is a stewardship for your future ministry.

Though the musical training and experience is important, please remember that a call to worship ministry is really a call to work with people, not music. Sometimes worship leaders can be enamored by their love for music, musical instruments or even music technology. These should not be

Section I: Considering Worship Ministry

the main focus of a healthy worship ministry. People should be the main focus. A call to worship ministry leads to caring for the souls of those on the worship teams and the congregation of your church. If you are called to any type of ministry, you need to have a love for people. A major focus of being a church is how we love one another. Twenty-three times in the New Testament we are commanded to love one another. As ministers we must set the example by loving the church as Christ loves the church. Music plays a role in worship ministry, but the priority in worship ministry is loving and caring for your people.

Do you have a strong desire to help others grow in their walk with Christ? This is a major part of a calling to ministry. Paul tells us in Colossians, "Him we proclaim, warning everyone and teaching everyone with all wisdom, that we may present everyone mature in Christ. For this I toil, struggling with all his energy that he powerfully works within me" (Col 1:28–29). The role of the minister is to present everyone mature in Christ, or in other words to disciple those in your ministry. In Ephesians Paul discusses the offices of the church (apostle, prophet, evangelist, shepherd, and teacher). The task of these ministry leaders is to "equip the saints for the work of ministry, for building up the body of Christ" (Eph 4:12). Even in worship ministry we teach and disciple. Worship ministers should carry out this equipping role in their weekly rehearsals and small group meetings. We also teach through songs used in congregational settings. If you are called to ministry, you are called to teach and disciple.

If you are called to ministry, do you meet the qualifications of an elder as explained in 1 Timothy 3 or Titus 1? Do you have the godly character required of those who lead in the church? Here is a quick listing of the characteristics of an elder from Titus 1: "husband of one wife, children are believers, a steward of God, not arrogant, not quick tempered, not a drunkard, not violent, not greedy for gain, hospitable, lover of good, self-controlled, upright, holy, disciplined, holds firm to the Word of God, gives instruction in sound doctrine, respectable, not a recent convert and well thought of by outsiders." Not all churches consider the worship ministry position an elder position, but those who serve as worship leaders should still have the same qualities of an elder. If you are called to worship ministry, you must be a person of godly character and integrity.

When considering a call to worship ministry another important confirmation of that call is when the pastors and lay people of your church believe and affirm that you could be an effective minister in the church. In

1 Timothy 5:22, Paul instructs Timothy to not "be hasty in the laying on of hands." Simply stated, church leaders should not hurry in their affirmation of new church leaders. Determining God's call on a potential minister comes after much time and observation of the potential minister. The leadership of your church should qualify you for ministry after witnessing your commitment to Christ, your character, your dependability, and your leadership skills. This highlights the importance of a potential ministry person to be involved in the local church. The church is the proving ground for your call to ministry. Students who plan to attend the school where I teach need a church affirmation statement as they apply. Their local church must affirm their call to ministry and recommend them for ministry preparation. Our school application also includes three character references completed by those who have knowledge of this person's life and ministry. If you are called to worship ministry, it will show in your love and service for the church. Those contemplating God's call to worship ministry must let this call mature as they serve their local church.

One other confirmation of God's calling on your life has to do with perseverance. The ministry can be a difficult place and a challenging calling. We see this demonstrated in the short chapter of 2 Corinthians 4. Here Paul mentions twice, in verses 1 and 16, that the Christian minister should not lose heart. He reminds us that in perseverance our power is not in our own weak efforts but in a powerful God when he states, "But we have this treasure in jars of clay, to show the surpassing power belongs to God and not to us. We are afflicted in every way, but not crushed; perplexed, but not driven to despair; persecuted, but not forsaken; struck down, but not destroyed; always carrying in the body the death of Jesus, so that the life of Jesus may also be manifested in our bodies" (2 Cor 4:7–11).

Ministers help their people walk through many perplexing life situations. Though worship ministry is rewarding, it does require a person to have a compelling desire to serve. Those called to ministry must have this strong desire so when things become intense in ministry they will not give up. It is often said with humor that ministers should never resign on a Monday. After a long Sunday of ministry among the people and dealing with complicated interpersonal issues, a minister may often think on Monday about doing something else. Spurgeon said the first sign of God's call to ministry is "an intense, all-absorbing desire for the work."[1] A call to ministry means a call to commitment for the long haul through the good

---

1. Spurgeon, *Lectures to My Students*, 26.

days of ministry and the difficult days. Other ministers used to tell me that if a person could choose to do anything else besides ministry, he should pursue that option; but if a person's calling and passion is for ministry, then be prepared to persevere.

How can a person know if they are called to worship ministry? Answering these questions should help you clarify your calling to ministry.

- Do you feel a compulsion to do ministry more than anything else?
- Has God given you the necessary gifts to do worship ministry?
- Are you willing to do the preparation and training needed to be an effective worship minister?
- Do you love working with people?
- Do you have the gifts to teach and disciple?
- Do you meet the qualifications of an elder listed in 1 Timothy 3 and Titus 1?
- Do your pastors and other leaders in the church affirm your calling and encourage you to press forward in training?
- Do you have the perseverance necessary to carry out ministry in the church?

CHAPTER 2

A Call to Worship Ministry Is a Call to Prepare

Those called to worship ministry need to be equipped. Calling leads to equipping. There is more than one way to equip for ministry but preparation is a must. Young ministers are often so impatient to get started in ministry that they bypass the necessary preparation. We have come through a period of time in our churches where a person who has a calling to be a worship minister need only have some vocal skills and the ability to accompany himself on a guitar or keyboard. Though these leaders may demonstrate giftedness, their equipping can be limited. Churches that open the door for these worship leaders to serve frequently find that the effectiveness of the worship leader is short-lived due to inexperience and lack of training. If a worship minister intends to serve in ministry for a lifetime, why would this person not take a small portion of that time to prepare and train?

The Apostle Paul believed that equipping others to do ministry was one of his major roles as a missionary to the churches. This is clearly seen in his letters to Timothy. In 2 Timothy 3:14–17, Paul reminds Timothy to:

> Continue in what you have learned and have firmly believed, knowing from whom you learned it and how from childhood you have been acquainted with the sacred writings, which are able to make you wise for salvation through faith in Christ Jesus. All Scripture is breathed out by God and profitable for teaching, for reproof, for correction, and for training in righteousness, that the man of God may be complete, equipped for every good work.

Section I: Considering Worship Ministry

As a person prepares for ministry, the leadership of the church has the responsibility to equip this young minister just as the Apostle Paul sought to equip Timothy. The church is the training ground for equipping young ministers. There should be no "Lone Ranger" worship leaders who have a solo worship-leading ministry floating around from one worship venue to another. The local church is the initial training station for newly called ministers.

Those called to worship ministry should seek out additional training in colleges and seminaries that will partner with the church in the equipping stage. Most churches can help recently called worship ministers with pastoral skills but are usually poorly equipped to help them develop the musical and worship-leading skills that are needed to be effective. What sort of skills can a Christian educational institution encourage in a newly called worship minister? During the education process there should be two major areas of study: music and theology. Worship ministers may already have musical talents but need to sharpen their music skills through a serious sequence of music studies. The worship minister also needs a thorough background in theological studies. This starts on the undergraduate level and continues in graduate studies at seminary. Young worship ministers should keep in mind that preparing for ministry on the front end of their ministry gives them a great foundation for years of effective ministry.

During this preparation period in college and seminary, the worship minister continues serving in the church, receiving supervision from a pastor and gaining experience working with people. Classroom study, practice of music skills, and experience serving in the church all combine to mature the newly called worship minister and to adequately prepare this person for years of fruitful service to Christ's church.

In this equipping stage for the worship minister, what sorts of skills need to be cultivated? Here is a partial list of knowledge and skills a worship minister should acquire to be an effective minister:

- Understanding the important truths of Scripture
- Understanding worship practice in Scripture
- Understanding the chief doctrines of the Christian faith
- Understanding church history especially as it relates to worship practice
- Understanding historical worship music in the church

A Call to Worship Ministry Is a Call to Prepare

- Understanding the worship leader's role in the church and on a church staff
- Developing people skills—ability to teach, disciple, and care for those who serve in the worship ministry under your leadership
- Developing worship planning skills
- Developing platform worship leadership skills—sensitivity to speaking, singing, reading Scripture, and praying in worship
- Developing wisdom for selecting worship songs for a congregation
- Developing administrative skills—ability to do calendar planning and plan rehearsals
- Developing communication skills—ability to help your worship teams to be fully informed of plans on an annual, monthly, and weekly basis
- Developing music-reading skills—ability to quickly understand and interpret written music in a rehearsal or service
- Developing aural skills—ability to hear and analyze music in a rehearsal or service (hearing intervals, chord progressions, tonalities, rhythms)
- Developing sight-singing skills—ability to view a line of music and perform the notes and rhythm fairly accurately without relying on a keyboard or other instrument
- Developing vocal skills—practicing healthy vocal technique and teaching these skills to vocalists in the church
- Developing keyboard or guitar skills—ability to accompany yourself in a rehearsal or worship service
- Developing arranging skills—ability to arrange worship songs for your church and write a lead sheet (notes, rhythms, chords) and vocal parts for a praise team or choir
- Developing instrumental skills—ability to work with instrumentalists and understand basic instrumental techniques
- Developing conducting skills—ability to direct a choir or instrumental group
- Developing technological skills—ability to work with sound systems, projection software, worship-planning software, and lighting and recording systems

Section I: Considering Worship Ministry

This list may seem daunting, but these skills are called upon almost every week as the worship minister serves in the local church. When a worship minister seeks out training, much of it will be introductory. A school will not be able to teach a student everything needed for ministry in the church. Although much of a worship leader's preparation may seem substantial in the early years, training should also be ongoing. Worship leaders should never stop growing in knowledge, wisdom, and skills as they serve the church. The effective worship minister embarks upon a lifetime of learning.

Electricians, plumbers, and mechanics must all go through an apprenticeship process before commencing their new work. Can you imagine an engineer, medical doctor, or lawyer who would bypass the important preparation period to move straight into work? Most churches expect their pastors to have the proper training to lead the church before being considered for the role of pastor. Worship ministers should also go through a time of preparation to be adequately equipped to serve the church. Preparation for one's life work is always a wise endeavor.

Has the Lord called you into worship ministry? How adequately prepared are you for this work? Are you currently serving in your church? Do you need to seek out further training at a college or seminary? A call to serve is a call to get equipped. The church will benefit from the preparation the worship minister diligently seeks and acquires. Preparation is not selfishly just for the worship minister but also unselfishly for the congregations this person serves for the many years to come.

CHAPTER 3

A Blueprint for Worship Ministry

I AM ALWAYS AMAZED at those who can take a blueprint and build a house according to the plans. How would a builder construct a home without a blueprint? Can you imagine the finished product? Would it be a safe home for a family? Having a philosophy of worship ministry for your church is similar to having a blueprint. A philosophy of worship ministry is an overall design and guide used to assist worship ministers as they build the ministry from the foundation up.

Obviously, one of the main tasks of the worship minister is to plan and lead congregational worship. But what drives that planning and leading? What are the parameters that guide the worship minister in the work of ministry to the church? Why do we do what we do? What are the principles that help us prioritize the week-to-week work of the worship ministry?

A healthy worship ministry is built around these four guiding principles: *exalt the Lord, edify the saints, equip people for ministry,* and *evangelize those outside of the church with the gospel.* Just like a blueprint gives direction on a building project, these principles give direction to the worship ministry as it grows and develops.

EXALT THE LORD

Is music in worship just a tool to share the message of the gospel? Many see music in worship as a pragmatic way to teach or prepare worshipers for the sermon. Music is a tool, but it is much more than that. Worship music is our personal offering given to glorify our great God. It is a sacrifice of praise.

Section I: Considering Worship Ministry

Hebrews 13:15 reminds us that we should "offer up a sacrifice of praise, the fruit of lips that acknowledge his name." In 1 Peter 2:5, Christians are told to offer spiritual sacrifices acceptable to God through Jesus Christ. Our primary purpose in worship ministry is to bring glory to God. The psalmist says, "O magnify the Lord with me, and let us exalt his name together" (Ps 34:3). We are also instructed to "exalt the Lord our God, and worship at his holy hill: for holy is the Lord God" (Ps 99:9). The prophet Isaiah says, "I will exalt Thee; I will give thanks to Thy name; for Thou has worked wonders, plans formed long ago with perfect faithfulness" (Isa 25:1). We offer our worship music to the Lord "so that in all things God may be glorified through Jesus Christ, to whom belongs the glory and dominion forever and ever, Amen" (1 Pet 4:11).

Worship leaders must keep their focus on God's glory and remember that God does not share his glory. It is all about him. The psalmist states, "Not to us, O Lord, not to us, but to your name give glory, for the sake of your steadfast love and faithfulness" (Ps 115:1). All of our efforts in worship ministry begin with the priority of exalting the Lord.

As we remember this truth concerning God's glory, this motivates us to strive for excellence in our efforts to exalt him. As we serve, we should constantly endeavor to improve the level of excellence in our ministry. We also teach our teams about humility and service so that God alone receives the glory. Each week that we meet for rehearsal or congregational worship the worship leader strives to help the people get a glimpse of the great God we praise.

EDIFY THE SAINTS

When we study the Epistles, we see a strong emphasis on the edification of the church. One of our main goals as worship ministers is for us to encourage and build up the believers. In 1 Corinthians 14 we read about principles for church gatherings, our congregational meetings. After a number of exhortations the Apostle Paul summarizes his thoughts by instructing us to let all things be done for edification (1 Cor 14:26). In Romans we are told to "pursue the things which make for peace and building up of one another" (Rom 14:19). We are also encouraged to teach and admonish in our gatherings with psalms, hymns, and spiritual songs (Col 3:16).

Christians are bombarded all week with discouraging words and events. When we gather to worship on the Lord's Day exalting the Lord, there should also be a strong horizontal element that encourages and builds up the body of Christ. As worship planners we can do much of this by selecting songs that edify, teach, and admonish our people.

We not only strive for edification in our congregational worship but also in our meetings during the week, such as worship band or choir rehearsals. Worship ministers have a great responsibility to minister to those in their weekly rehearsals. An edifying worship ministry will encourage the building of relationships, leading people to feel wanted and loved.

EQUIP FOR MINISTRY

Are we equipping others to do worship ministry? Another of the important tasks for worship ministers is to train people to do what they do. Some worship ministers find themselves doing almost all of the tasks of ministry themselves without engaging others to assist. It is much healthier for your church (though often more work for you) to bring others alongside and train them for ministry. In Ephesians the Apostle Paul says that the main task of ministers is to "equip the saints for the work of ministry" (Eph 4:11–14). The paid ministers on staff should not be doing the entire ministry of the church. Who are the worship leaders, vocalists, and instrumentalists in the next generation? Who are you equipping for future ministry? We most definitely need to be equipping the next generation as well as other generations in the church.

How do we equip the saints in worship ministry? Discipleship should be the first priority as we work with our worship teams, whether the team is a choir, children's group, or worship band. We also disciple our congregations as we select great lyrics to sing in worship. The worship minister must be intentional about discipleship, determining ways to teach biblical truth to our teams.

We also equip our worship teams musically in rehearsals as we use the teachable moments when learning songs. We equip musically by providing training opportunities for children, students, and adults. Perhaps we organize a music academy in our church that offers private vocal and instrumental lessons to our people.

A worship leader shared with me a while back that he would like to find five or six talented musicians to help with the worship ministry at his church each week and not bother trying to include others. This team would learn to work well together and provide an excellent level of worship music

Section I: Considering Worship Ministry

all of the time. It could be that in some small churches this number of musically skilled people would be all you could find to serve in the worship ministry, but many churches have the capability of involving many others in worship ministry. This worship leader's philosophy of worship ministry was based on the idea of "less is more."

When considering the challenges of equipping believers to do ministry, the "less is more" philosophy is not a biblically based philosophy. What it should be is "more is more." How much influence can we as worship ministers have each week in equipping others? We have more influence by involving more people on our worship teams. Plan to rotate members of the worship band and vocal teams from Sunday to Sunday. If your church does not have a choir, consider beginning one so that many others can participate in the worship ministry at your church. This also gives the worship minister the opportunity to disciple more believers through worship ministry.

What happens to the worship ministry when you are no longer able to lead? Have you equipped others to do your work? What happens in our churches when worship ministers fail to equip new generations?

EVANGELIZE WITH THE GOSPEL

Jesus commanded us to go and make disciples when he gave us the Great Commission in Matthew 28:18–20. We want to edify and equip the saints, but we also need to evangelize the lost. What better tool is there to share the gospel than a well-written song that explains the gospel or a song that shares a testimony of a changed life? Seasonal musicals can be an effective tool of evangelism as those who do not know Christ attend these events. Worship ministry should support the outreach and mission programs of the church. We should involve our worship teams on mission trips, using music as a tool of sharing the gospel.

As we keep a focus on evangelism through our worship ministry, it also helps leaders keep a gospel-centered focus in all that we do in the area of worship. We need a gospel-centered, cross-centered emphasis in our song selection, in our worship planning, in our rehearsal leadership, and in our one-on-one relationships.

The worship ministry of your church should fit well into the overall vision and goals of the church. It is not an island unto itself. How does the worship ministry of your church support and meet the vision and goals of the total church ministry?

You can see this basic philosophy of worship ministry in these four paradigms: *exalt the Lord*, *edify the saints*, *equip for ministry*, and *evangelize with the gospel*. How does having a blueprint or philosophy of worship ministry such as the one just shared impact the vision and planning of the worship minister? Without a philosophy guiding the minister, it is easy to find yourself going down side roads or trying to travel too many roads at one time. A worship ministry blueprint helps the minister sort out what things need to be a priority and what things are good but probably not a priority. If the task or new idea does not fit the worship ministry philosophy, perhaps you should consider not doing that particular task. As you make plans for the worship ministry at your church, seek to discover if your plans carry out at least one of the main purposes for worship ministry.

CHAPTER 4

Getting Started in Worship Ministry

CHURCHES LOOKING FOR A worship minister want someone who has experience. The challenge for new worship leaders is how to get this experience. The primary place to gain experience for those called to vocational ministry is in the local church. Young aspiring worship leaders may begin by volunteering to lead student worship services or serve in the worship band as the bass guitar player or sing in the choir. These are great starting places to gain experience and to demonstrate dependability and commitment to ministry. Those who are called to ministry need church leaders to affirm their calling. These leaders need to see potential ministers in action week to week. Many churches today seek to train their own ministers from those who show calling and ability in their congregations. Being a faithful steward is a starting place for inexperienced worship leaders. It takes patience to wait on the Lord to open doors of opportunity rather than trying to pry those doors open yourself. Ministry experience begins when a person willingly agrees to serve humbly with integrity in a place of ministry no matter how big or small the job is.

ORDINATION

The "seal of approval" for a person called to ministry is ordination. In Acts and the Epistles, local church congregations would often set apart a person for ministry (Acts 6:3; 13:2–3; 1 Tim 4:14; 5:22). This action comes after the person has demonstrated a strong knowledge of Scripture, an evidence of a fruitful life in Christ, a lifestyle of holiness, a spiritual maturity in decision-making, a love for serving people, an unshakeable integrity, and a personal awareness of a call to ministry. Church leaders need time to observe and determine if a person seeking ordination should be ordained. Often churches will wait until a person has finished college or seminary to consider ordination.

Should a worship minister seek ordination? As discussed earlier, a worship minister is a minister first. Those called to vocational ministry should be affirmed by their home churches or the churches where they are serving. This affirmation is ordination. When full-time worship ministry positions began to appear in churches, it was not common for the worship minister to be ordained. Student ministers, children's ministers, and other staff-level positions often were not ordained since they were seen as directors of ministries rather than pastors of the church. This view slowly changed and now it is a usual practice for a worship minister to seek ordination.

The ordination process varies depending on the church and denomination. In the Baptist tradition, a worship minister may ask the pastor of his home church or the church he is currently serving to consider ordaining him. If the pastor and other leaders of the church agree that this person demonstrates calling, spiritual maturity, and skills needed for ministry, they will move forward by scheduling an ordination council. The council usually consists of other ordained ministers from that church or other area pastors who are like-minded. The ordination council typically meets on a Saturday morning or a Sunday afternoon for a couple of hours where the candidate shares about his conversion and calling then answers questions on a variety of theological and ministry topics. If the candidate successfully satisfies the council with his answers, the candidate moves forward to the actual ordination service. Usually held on a Sunday evening, the ordination service consists of the candidate giving his testimony and calling to ministry before the congregation and an ordination sermon given by the pastor of the church or another influential pastor that has been a mentor to the new minister. A charge is given to the candidate, followed by a time of special prayer for the candidate. This usually involves the candidate (and perhaps wife) kneeling at the front of the church while other ordained ministers and deacons offer prayers for the candidate. The church then gives the candidate a certificate of ordination.

An ordained minister is considered differently by the U.S. government than other employees of a church for tax purposes. The ordained minister is seen as a self-employed worker, which changes the way he pays for Social

Security. Currently, the ordained minister is also able to get his housing allowance tax free (does not include Social Security). There are many tax considerations an ordained minister should consider. Wise counsel should be sought from an expert who understands ministers and tax law.

In the conservative evangelical tradition, ordination is reserved for men since these churches see ordained ministers as pastoral positions. Scripture allows only men to serve in positions of pastoral authority in the church. This does not discount the work of women in ministry. God calls women to ministry in the local church as well.

SO CAN A WOMAN SERVE AS A WORSHIP MINISTER?

This question arises often where I teach because we have women in our undergraduate and graduate worship programs. As discussed earlier, if a church sees the worship minister role as a pastoral role then Scripture would teach that it is a role for a man to fill. In a large majority of conservative evangelical churches I do see the worship ministry position being viewed as a pastoral position only for men. In the churches where I served as worship minister this was the view.

Some churches, however, may not view the worship ministry role as pastoral and approach the position more as a music director. In my opinion a church with this view makes allowance for a man or woman to serve in the position. Some churches may see the lead pastor as an elder who provides pastoral coverage for anyone serving on the platform in a service. Often there may even be a young man serving in a staff position who is too inexperienced to be considered for a pastoral role and the lead pastor provides elder oversight for his work. Many larger churches have one or two associate worship ministry roles that work under the leadership of the worship minister. It is common to see women serving in these associate roles. I believe God calls men and women into vocational ministry, but how those roles work out in the worship area are best defined by the local church leadership rather than making a blanket statement that only men should serve in worship ministry roles.

While every church has to decide what roles women should fill in the church, no church should ignore the invaluable contribution that women provide in worship. Their gifts and passions for worship need a place in corporate worship and the corporate worship experience needs them. A woman's presence and voice on the platform represents at least half of the congregation, sometimes more. The sight and sound of women in worship completes the picture of the created order. God created them male and female and he created them both to worship.[1]

INTERVIEWING WITH A CHURCH

Upon completion of a college or seminary degree, ministers are eager to serve a church. For me after finishing seminary it meant returning to a church where I interned for a summer while in college. The church asked me to return as their full-time worship and student minister. Unless you are in one of the denominations that place new ministers in churches, things work differently as you seek a worship position. It is possible that your home church may be in need of a worship minister and will talk with you. Of course, prayer is the first place to begin seeking the Lord's guidance as to where to serve. Today many ministers will post their resumes on denominational websites, seminary placement sites, or some other website that collects resumes for churches to view. It can be fairly confusing when a minister gets calls from several churches all looking for a worship minister.

Before you begin talking to a church seeking a worship minister, there are several things you need to decide. First, what type of church do you think is best suited for your abilities? What is your skill set when it comes to leading worship? Some ministers will seek to work in a certain region of the country because of family needs or culture. Based on your theological foundations, what churches would you consider or not consider? How is the church governed? Is the church you are considering a congregationally led church, elder led, or denominationally led? What are the first priority principles you would seek in a church? What other principles do you prefer but are not required?

There are many considerations you should contemplate before talking with any churches. This will help to narrow the focus in your search for a ministry position. When looking at a church position, one of the most important factors to consider is the senior pastor. What do you know about the senior pastor? How well did he and the former worship minister work together? What are the pastor's theological views? What is his philosophy of ministry and leadership style? What is his vision for the church? What are his expectations for staff members? How does he view worship? Is he

---

[1]. I am grateful for some insights on this topic of women in worship ministry from Dr. Scott Connell, worship coordinator at Boyce College, Louisville, Kentucky.

interested in working closely with the worship minister on worship planning? Does he view the ministry staff as a team or is he more of a benevolent dictator?

One quick sign of the pastor's leadership is how involved he is in the search process. Is all of the communication concerning the worship position coming from a committee person? It is healthy for lay people to be involved in the selection process but not a good sign when the pastor is uninvolved. Why would a pastor let a committee choose a candidate for the worship ministry position when this staff person will probably work most closely with him on a daily basis? The pastor should have a vested interest in choosing a worship minister and be involved in the process.

When a worship minister begins to talk seriously with a church about a possible worship ministry position, there should also be some long discussions with the pastor. These discussions should help the person seeking the position to discern how well the pastor–worship minister relationship can be. If you do not think you can serve with the pastor of an inquiring church, you should not continue discussions with the church. Perhaps the most miserable of church positions is where a worship minister serves but cannot work well with the pastor. The pastor and worship minister should be a team united in service to the church. It does not take long for the church to see if this relationship is healthy.

In the initial stages of talking with a search committee several things can happen. Sometimes there is a phone or video interview with the candidate and the search committee. This is usually a "get acquainted" session aimed at both parties discovering more about each other. The committee will have a number of questions for the candidate. It is also helpful for the candidate to write down in advance some questions to pose to the committee. Everything does not have to be discovered in this first interview.

In these early discussions it is not wise to ask about salary. A worship minister can give a search committee the impression that he is more interested in the salary than in serving. Let the committee bring this up first. Once they mention the salary details, then it is acceptable to ask some questions that pertain to salary. The salary discussion will probably not happen in the early interviews. Sometimes a church will advertise the salary amount in a classified ad on a website or denominational paper. It would be helpful for the worship minister to estimate a potential family budget and know what salary amount can meet this budget.

Churches sometimes offer a new worship minister a salary package that includes base pay, housing allowance, health insurance, life insurance, and retirement compensation. As a minister considers going to a church, it is helpful once again to seek out wise counsel from a knowledgeable person who understands ministers' salaries. New worship ministers are often enamored by the total amount a church is offering to pay. The salary amount may seem large to a person who has been in school working part-time jobs. A more realistic view of a total salary amount is seen when subtracting health insurance costs and other items that need to be deducted such as taxes and retirement savings. There should also be some consideration of the cost of housing in the new ministry setting. Once these amounts are subtracted, the minister may discover that the salary being offered by the church actually will not support the minister's family needs. No one goes into ministry for the money, but it is good if the church can help meet a minister's basic needs. Some churches can only offer a certain salary amount due to the size of the congregation or the economic situation of the church community. At this point a worship minister needs to seek the Lord for clear guidance about this church. Before going to a new ministry any concerns about salary should be discussed and settled.

If a search committee does not offer a job description, the worship minister should ask for one. This document is helpful to clarify expectations for this ministry. It is also helpful to ask for a copy of the church's budget, constitution and bylaws, and other personnel policies. The church's budget shows its priorities. How much budget money has the church allotted for worship ministry expenses? Often churches have to budget so much to create a worship ministry position that there are insufficient funds remaining to be used for resources in the worship ministry. It is much easier to explore these questions or concerns in this early stage of discussion than after you are called to the church.

After several interviews by phone or video, the church may ask the worship minister and spouse to visit. Often the initial visit is more "discovery" and not about meeting the congregation. The church should take care of all travel expenses. The search committee sets up several meetings, including time with the pastor. This will help the prospective minister get to know the church and community. If the relationship progresses, the church then asks the minister to come back "in view of a call," which means they will present this minister to the congregation. The candidate is asked to lead worship and usually given an opportunity for a question-and-answer time with the congregation. If this goes well, the church takes a congregational vote to determine whether to call you as worship minister.

If the worship minister has serious concerns about going to this church to serve on staff, the process needs to be slowed down. Churches should not have a candidate come in view of a call if the candidate has major reservations about serving that church. It is difficult on a church if members vote to offer a call and then the worship minister declines. If the church is moving too fast, the worship minister should consider asking the search committee to give more time for prayer and seeking wise counsel.

Going to serve a new church as a worship minister can be a daunting decision to make. Worship ministers should keep in mind that there is no perfect church. Every church has struggles, even the ones that appear to have all things running well. Ultimately, when considering a new ministry setting it is helpful to keep the focus on the big picture. Is the Lord leading you to this church? Is the church theologically sound? Is the pastor someone you could support and find joy serving alongside? Are you equipped to meet the music and worship needs of this church? Is the church able to support your family financially? These are the big picture questions. Facilities, equipment, resources, and other details come into play with the decision but should not be the final determiners.

After spending some soul-searching time in prayer and talking with mentors who know you and your abilities, there comes the time when the worship minister has to take a step of faith towards the new ministry. There are still many unknowns plus the sadness of leaving where you currently serve, but the Lord is good. He will confirm your steps after you take the initial step of faith.

SECTION II

Leading the Worship Ministry

CHAPTER 5

Working with Your Pastor

ONE OF THE KEY relationships for the worship minister is with the senior pastor. Hopefully this relationship works well as you both serve the church. Over the years I served on a number of church staffs with a number of pastors. These pastors were all different in temperament and leadership styles yet effective leaders for the churches.

Jesus is the chief shepherd of the church (1 Pet 5:1–5) and as the pastor serves the local church he is under-shepherd to Jesus. The pastor is ultimately responsible for the spiritual health of the body of believers he leads. He is ultimately the main worship leader for the church. The senior pastor's work is a great responsibility requiring constant attention. Because of the pastor's role in the church, worship ministers must be comfortable coming under the pastor's authority. The worship minister comes alongside the pastor and supports him in his efforts to lead and care for the church. A healthy relationship with your pastor takes time, sensitivity, humility, unselfishness, and prayer.

PRAY FOR YOUR PASTOR

We can get so busy in the work of the ministry that we do not take time to pray. Prayer should precede ministry. One of the areas of our prayer life must include praying for our pastor. A worship minister can fall into a trap of being critical of the pastor while not even praying for him. When I am irritated or disappointed with my pastor, if I pray for him the Lord changes my heart towards him. We need to be lifting up our pastors in prayer every day. The church, the pastor, staff, and other leaders are in a spiritual battle each day. This battle requires spiritual weapons (Eph 6:10–20). Prayer is one those key weapons.

Our pastors need prayer for wisdom as they lead the church. They need prayer for strength as they are constantly in a ministry mode. They need prayer for their families that they are effective leaders in the home. They need prayer for the battle against sexual temptations as so many pastors can fail in this area. How much prayer time do you spend for your pastor? Make this a top priority.

DO NOT LET YOUR PASTOR BE SURPRISED

U.S. President Harry Truman used to have a sign on his desk that said, "The buck stops here." President Truman was keenly aware that he was the one who took the credit or blame for the health and well-being of the nation. Pastors feel this weight of responsibility for the church, including things that happen under the guidance of one his staff members. As a worship minister one of the goals in my relationship with my pastor is to not let him be surprised.

Over a period of time, a worship minister can build trust with the pastor by demonstrating good planning and communication. There is a fine line between doing your job as a worship minister and consulting with your pastor before launching into new directions. The pastor does not want you to consult with him on everyday decisions that you as the worship minister should make. However, the pastor does want to know when you are making plans for something new in the worship ministry area. After we pray seeking the Lord's vision in our worship ministry, we should communicate with our pastor and seek his wise counsel.

Since the pastor is ultimately responsible even for the worship ministry, worship ministers must seek to keep the pastor informed in advance of anything that could end up "on his desk." Sometimes in discussions with lay people I would discover their discontent about some aspect of the worship ministry. I would, of course, attempt to help them work through their feelings and offer some resolution, but I would also quickly tell my pastor about the conversation. Sometimes the next step of this situation involved the lay person going to the pastor to relate something I did or did not do. I want to address the situation with my pastor before he hears it from someone else.

As worship ministers we should often ask ourselves, "Is there anything I need to tell my pastor that he does not know so he won't be surprised?" Communication can make or break your relationship with your pastor. The ability or lack of ability to effectively communicate to the pastor, staff, and church can cause a worship leader to sink or swim in ministry.

BE A FRIEND

The ministry can be a very lonely place for a pastor. As a minister there are things you know about church matters that you cannot share with a church member. Pastors can carry heavy burdens for their people as they counsel and pray for them. Worship ministers should not only think of their pastor as the boss, but also seek to build a relationship with him as a friend. If you are a male worship leader, try to find time to be with your pastor away from the church. This could be some recreational activity (golf, running, going to a baseball game). Consider having a lunch meal together, and do not always talk about church details or issues. Seek to find out how he is doing and ask about his family.

One year when I traveled to a music conference, my pastor came along to spend some time with me but also to have his own study time while I was in the conference sessions. Another time of the year the ministerial staff at my church would go away for a couple of retreat days. The retreat schedule was loosely planned, so it majored on relationship building and not just planning and resolving problems. This kind of environment creates a peaceful staff supportive to the pastor.

SPEAK WELL OF YOUR PASTOR

Because I respect the position the Lord gives my pastor as the chief under-shepherd of the church, I never want to be critical of him with church members or others outside my church. We may not always agree on everything, but I will be supportive to him, speaking kind things about him to others. Pastors are not perfect people. They make mistakes just like worship ministers make mistakes. If I could not be supportive to my pastor, I would pray for the Lord to either change my heart or move me to another place of ministry. The only time this would be different is if my pastor had done something illegal or immoral or was teaching something contrary to Scripture.

Do you take opportunities to say an encouraging word about your pastor from the platform or in front of church people? In love, build him up in your speech.

SERVE YOUR PASTOR

How can you serve your pastor? We can begin by ensuring he has adequate time to preach each week through thoughtful worship planning. As worship ministers plan their services, special attention should be given to the timing of each element of worship. Pastors should not be worried about their sermon running over the allotted time. Seek to find out how much time he needs each week, and be thoughtful as you plan the front portion of the service. In your worship planning, strive to prepare the hearts of the congregation to hear God's Word preached through thoughtful selection of songs and Scripture.

Worship ministers serve their pastors by following through on commitments and responsibilities he gives them. Make time to listen when he wants to talk. Let his oversight of your ministry bring him joy and not grief. The Apostle Peter writes in 1 Peter 5:5 for the younger Christians in the church to be subject to the elders. He instructs all in the body of Christ to clothe themselves with great humility toward one another, for "God opposes the proud but gives grace to the humble." As we serve our pastors, let us do this with great humility.

SUMMARY

- As you serve your church seek to excel in your relationship with the pastor.
- Pray for your pastor
- Do not let your pastor be surprised
- Be a friend
- Speak well of your pastor
- Serve your pastor

CHAPTER 6

The Daily Life of the Worship Leader

THOSE WHO LEAD OTHERS in worship on Sundays must be diligent to abide in Christ during the week. Why is this crucial for the worship leader? A worship leader can appear to be an effective leader but be devoid of the strength of Jesus that comes from abiding in him. Authentic worship leaders must walk with Christ not just on Sunday but every day. When we are not walking with Christ daily, we drift and fall into sin. There is no middle ground. Drifting and falling into sin hinders or even disqualifies us from effectively leading others to worship Christ. This seems very obvious, yet many worship leaders still neglect their walk with Christ throughout the week.

John chapter 15 reminds us of the importance of abiding in Christ as a daily practice. The first step is to acknowledge our weakness to live a life pleasing to God outside of daily abiding in Christ. We can do nothing of lasting eternal value outside of our abiding in Christ. Not only is Jesus our vine that gives us sustenance, but we are also reminded in John that he is our living bread and living water. The Apostle Paul recognized this truth when he wrote that Jesus' power is made strong in our weakness—when I am weak, Christ is strong (2 Cor 12: 9–10). We are weak vessels and utterly dependent on the work of Christ in our lives daily. John 15 also reminds us that we do not create or sustain the fruit in our lives or the lives of others. Jesus produces the fruit in us when we abide in him. The fruit is a byproduct of our abiding in the vine. When we are abiding in Christ, there will be fruit and this is the sign of a disciple of Jesus.

Section II: Leading the Worship Ministry

After acknowledging our weakness and desperate reliance upon Christ, we then seek to give priority to spending time in God's Word daily. What is the amount of time we need to spend reading and meditating on God's Word each day—thirty minutes, one hour, two hours? How much time do we spend watching sports, movies, or other recreational activities? Jesus tells us that where our treasure is, there we will find our heart. Even our own busy ministry responsibilities can crowd out our time in God's Word. We must prioritize our time alone with the Lord in his Word and in prayer everyday.

Christians often segment their lives by thinking of their time in the Word as one slice of their week. Family time is another slice. Time working in our jobs takes another slice; then we have leisure time and time building relationships. Thinking of areas of our lives like slices of a pie gives us a false view of how abiding in Christ needs to take priority in our lives. *Our time with Christ is not one slice of the pie. It is the whole pie.* We abide in Christ by letting his strength permeate and impact all that we do. Abiding in Christ starts as we spend time in his Word and radiates out to every other area of our lives.

Practically speaking, how do ministers carve out time in their schedules to ensure good nourishment in God's Word and prayer on a daily basis? Is the best time in the early morning or late evening? Some ministers tend to function better in the early morning while others late at night. Perhaps the most important thought at this juncture is that you set a consistent time aside daily and make it a regular practice. My usual time in the Word is early in the morning while things are still quiet in the house. When my children were young, I tried to rise early before they got out of bed. Once my children were up, my attention needed to turn towards them. If you tend to function better in this area late at night, that is fine; however, it is still important that you take a few moments in the morning to get your heart right before the Lord and pray for your day. Reading a short Scripture passage and praying, even if it takes ten minutes, is better than moving into your day unprepared spiritually.

It is good if you have one spot in your home where you can sit, be quiet, and read the Scriptures. Developing a daily routine of doing this and being consistent in your routine can launch you into a lifetime of daily worship with the Lord. Everyone tends to struggle with crowded schedules, but for the worship minister this daily time alone with the Lord is *not an option*. If Jesus needed time alone with the Father (Matt 14:23; Luke 5:16);

how much more do we need to do this? You cannot spiritually nourish your people in the worship ministry or your congregation on Sunday if you are not being spiritually nourished. When we are not finding time alone with the Lord, we can become stagnant or even dry. The people at your church (and your family) come to your "well" for spiritual nourishment. Is your well stagnant or dry? You have probably heard this saying many times, but it is true: we minister out of the overflow of what God is doing in our lives. Your ministry and family need a well flowing with living water, which comes from God's Spirit doing a fresh work in your life as you spend time in his Word and in prayer.

After you establish a daily time and place, it is best if you have a plan for Bible reading and a thoughtful way to spend time in prayer. For the past few years I have been on a Bible reading plan that leads me once through the Old Testament and twice through the New Testament in a year. Each day there are approximately four chapters to read from the Old and New Testaments. I also keep a journal writing down helpful verses that stand out to me in that day's readings.

Following time in the Word, take time to commune with God in prayer. Consider keeping a prayer journal to help you remember prayer needs for your family and others with whom you minister. You might even write out your prayers. I would also encourage you to consider getting on a schedule of Scripture memory.

Hudson Taylor, the well-known English missionary to China in the nineteenth century, is known to have found time in the Word and prayer between 2 and 4 a.m. He was constantly around people all hours of the day and the middle of the night provided the only time he could be alone with the Lord. Taylor believed that the hardest part of a missionary career is to maintain regular, prayerful Bible study. "Satan will always find you something to do when you ought to be occupied about that, if it is only arranging a window blind."[1]

How are you abiding with Christ this week? What do you need to do to make your daily time with the Lord in his Word and in prayer a priority? Your congregation needs you to lead them each week in worship from an authentic daily walk with Christ. It is the work of Christ in your daily life that will encourage your people on Sunday as you lead them.

---

1. Taylor, *Hudson Taylor's Spiritual Secrets*, 239.

CHAPTER 7

Being Above Reproach

These are the generations of Noah. Noah was a righteous man, blameless in his generation. Noah walked with God.
Genesis 6:9

When Abram was ninety-nine years old the Lord appeared to Abram and said to him, "I am God Almighty; walk before me, and be blameless, that I may make my covenant between me and you, and may multiply you greatly.
Genesis 17:1–2

There was a man in the land of Uz whose name was Job, and that man was blameless and upright, one who feared God and turned away from evil.
Job 1:1

Be not wise in your own eyes; fear the Lord, and turn away from evil.
Proverbs 3:7

By steadfast love and faithfulness iniquity is atoned for, and by the fear of the Lord one turns away from evil.
Proverbs 16:6

THE OVERARCHING THEME IN these Old Testament passages concerns character. Noah, Abraham, and Job all had a common description concerning their character. They were blameless, righteous, upright, God-fearing men who turned away from evil, a demonstration of being above reproach. As a worship minister serving in the church, we must always seek to be above reproach. Our work is a holy work and deserves Christ-like leaders. Being above reproach according to the *Oxford English Dictionary* is to act in such a way that no criticism can be made—to be perfect.[1] I think the concept of being above reproach goes much deeper than this definition.

It seems that every month or so I hear of a minister who has fallen and is forced to leave the ministry. I do not believe ministers consciously set out to destroy their own ministries by falling into sinful habits or practices. It is a slow drift that can be imperceptible at first, yet takes a minister way off the path in a short while. Being above reproach is a constant fight on the part of the minister. We are in a spiritual battle for our ministries each day and if we do not recognize the spiritual warfare, we too will fall.

When thinking about how to be above reproach, Titus 1 is a good focal point. In verses 5–9 the Apostle Paul gives us a list of qualifications for elders in the church. Though every worship ministry position may not be considered an elder-type position, these verses should function as a checklist for the worship minister. Here is a quick listing of the characteristics of an elder: husband of one wife, children are believers, a steward of God, not arrogant, not quick tempered, not a drunkard, not violent, not greedy for gain, hospitable, lover of good, self-controlled, upright, holy, disciplined, holds firm to the Word of God, gives instruction in sound doctrine, respectable, not a recent convert, and well thought of by outsiders.

This list is really all about the *character* of the minister. The church leader must be free from sinful behaviors that would prevent him from being a Christ-like example for the congregation. The call to ministry is a call to holiness. From a book by John Stott we see a portion of a letter written in 1840 by Robert Murray McCheyne to the Rev. Dan Edwards, who was preparing to travel to Germany as a missionary to Jews. McCheyne, a well-known Scottish preacher, wrote:

> I trust you will have a pleasant and profitable time in Germany. I know you will apply hard to German; but do not forget the culture of the inner man,—I mean of the heart. How diligently the cavalry officer keeps his sabre clean and sharp; every stain he rubs off with the greatest care. Remember you are God's sword—His instrument—I trust a chosen vessel unto Him to bear His name. In great measure, according to the purity and perfections of the

---

1. https://en.oxforddictionaries.com/definition/reproach.

instrument, will be the success. It is not great talents God blesses so much as great likeness to Jesus. A holy minister is an awful weapon in the hand of God.[2]

Though no follower of Christ is without sin, those who are ministers in the church must be willing to live to the high standard that is set forth in Titus for an elder. People who will not live above reproach should not go into ministry. These were the thoughts of Charles Haden Spurgeon, renowned English preacher of the nineteenth century. Spurgeon said in a lecture to his ministry students:

> True and genuine piety is necessary as the first indispensible requisite [for ministry]. Whatever "call" a man may pretend to have, if he has not been called to holiness, he certainly has not been called to ministry.
>
> We are to stand equipped with the whole armor of God, ready for feats of valor not expected of others: to us self denial, self-forgetfulness, patience, perseverance, longsuffering, must be everyday virtues, and who is sufficient for these things? We had need live very near to God, if we would approve ourselves in our vocation.
>
> We have need of very vigorous piety, because our danger is so much greater than that of others.[3]

When ministers fall there are subsequent waves of hurt crashing on their families and congregations because "sin splatters." If you think your sin only affects you, this is far from the truth. It certainly impacts your relationship to the Lord and it can wound all of those who love you.

Here are a few guidelines for practicing being above reproach.

1. Seek constant nourishment from Scripture. Ministers who do not spend daily time in the Word are already drifting. It's a dangerous thing to think that we do not have time for God's Word in our ministries. One of the best ways to fight sin in your life is Bible intake. The greater the daily Bible intake the better you will be at fighting temptation and sin (Ps 119:11, 105).

2. Reserve time for prayer in your ministry. Perhaps the single most important influence we have as ministers is being a prayer warrior for our homes and ministries (Eph 6:18–19).

---

2 Stott, *Preacher's Portrait*, 120.

3. Spurgeon, *Lectures to My Students*, 9, 14–15.

3. Guard your heart. Proverbs 4:23 tells us to "keep your heart with all vigilance, for from it flow the springs of life." Be on the alert for improper thoughts or emotions we may have towards another church member or staff person. Never be alone with a person of the opposite sex that is not your spouse. Jerry Bridges warns that believers can be "drawn away from watchfulness by overconfidence. We come to believe we are beyond a particular temptation. We look at someone else's fall and say, 'I would never do that.'"[4] If you think you are strong and above temptation, you will be the first to fall (1 Cor 10:12–13).

4. Avoid the appearance of evil. Think about how an action or activity may appear to another church member or neighbor. It may be an innocent activity, but if it looks improper perhaps you should not be involved. Do not destroy your witness for something you think you have a right to do. This is being above reproach (1 Thess 5:22).

5. Run from places of temptation. You know how you are wired and where your weak areas are. If you are viewing pornography, you must escape this sin *immediately*. It will destroy you, your family, and your ministry. Put in safeguards that prevent you from slipping in this area (Heb 12:1–4). The Apostle Paul even warns us to be careful when helping a brother who has fallen lest we be tempted as well (Gal 6:1).

6. Get accountability. Sometimes ministers can be the loneliest people. We must have friends and build relationships with someone who can hold us accountable. Who is your accountability partner (Rom 1:8–15)?

7. Refuse to handle money at your church (1 Tim 6:6–10). Always get a trusted lay person to collect money or get money deposited. Do not be responsible for keeping money or checks for church activities. If you are allowed to use a church credit card, never, ever use that card for anything except official church business. Always keep receipts of all church expenses.

8. Do not let your gifting be a cover for poor character. Your gifting may be notable but in ministry it is nothing without your character. Character must always precede gifting.

Being above reproach is an impossible task outside of the work of Holy Spirit in our lives. I need to be reminded daily of how weak and desperate

---

4. Bridges, *Pursuit of Holiness*, 48.

Section II: Leading the Worship Ministry

I am in my own strength and how easily I can fall. We are called to be holy ministers for Christ. We cannot do this in our own strength. Every morning before we leave our homes we need to seek the Spirit's power to live the life of a minister that is above reproach. Your character impacts all that you are and do.

> Who shall ascend the hill of the Lord?
> And who shall stand in his holy place?
> He who has clean hands and a pure heart,
> who does not lift up his soul to what is false
> and does not swear deceitfully.
> He will receive blessing from the Lord
> and righteousness from the God of his salvation.
> Such is the generation of those who seek him,
> who seek the face of the God of Jacob. Selah.

Ps 24:3–6

CHAPTER 8

Loving People

WORSHIP MINISTRY IS ALL about the two great commandments: loving God and loving your neighbor or your congregation (Matt 22:34–40). For many years in ministry I had the title "minister of music." With this leadership position I often thought that I wasn't really a minister of music like my title said, but a minister to people. As worship ministers we can be distracted from loving our people like we should due to the demanding aspects of our work, such as planning, rehearsing, and leading worship several times a week. We spend energy focusing on the latest worship songs, discovering the best possible technology for worship services, and bringing vision and principles to the worship ministry. All of these good things must become secondary to caring for the souls of our people.

Those who serve in worship ministry often have a tendency to be introverted. It goes with the territory of being a musician. Making yourself available and open to the lay people in your ministry can be a challenge. Sometimes it is easier to not check on people and assume things are going well unless you hear differently. We must be proactive in our approach to the lay people in our ministry. We need to speak to them before and after services or rehearsals. We must ask how we can be praying for them. We need to deal with any conflict or potential conflict right away before it has the opportunity to fester. If you find yourself leaning in the direction of introversion, you must make every effort to break from that mold for the sake of your ministry. Be the first one to take the initiative to speak and seek to minister. Loving your people just as Jesus loves should motivate you to reach out.

Section II: Leading the Worship Ministry

As worship ministers we are shepherds to our people. The senior pastor of your church is the chief under shepherd but worship ministers must also take care of those who serve under their leadership in the worship ministry. 1 Peter 5:1–5 instructs us as leaders to exercise oversight with those in our ministries. We should serve them *willingly*, *eagerly*, and *by example*.

> So I exhort the elders among you, as a fellow elder and a witness of the sufferings of Christ, as well as a partaker in the glory that is going to be revealed: shepherd the flock of God that is among you, exercising oversight, not under compulsion, but willingly, as God would have you; not for shameful gain, but eagerly; not domineering over those in your charge, but being examples to the flock. And when the chief Shepherd appears, you will receive the unfading crown of glory. Likewise, you who are younger, be subject to the elders. Clothe yourselves, all of you, with humility toward one another, for "God opposes the proud but gives grace to the humble."

As we work with our worship teams week in and week out, we should care for them *willingly*, not under compulsion. We do not *have* to care for them; we *get* to care for them. We should seek God's wisdom in caring for the souls of our people. Do you have a practice of praying for those in your worship ministry weekly? Keep a list of your worship team members nearby as you spend time in prayer each day.

We should also show leadership with our people *eagerly*. They should know that we love them and desire to see them grow in their walk with Christ. We do not build our worship teams in order to make our ministries look successful or to show what great leaders we are. We do not lead out of greed. Our eagerness should indicate the joy of Christ to our people. This old saying is still true: "People don't care how much you know, until they know how much you care."

Worship ministers must lead *by example*. We are not dictators domineering over our worship teams. We should display servant leadership with Jesus as our model. Jesus was the perfect example of servant leadership. He washed his disciples' feet, including the feet of one who would betray him. What kind of example are you setting at rehearsals or other times your people are gathered? Do you take the initiative to meet a need of one of your lay people? Are you the first one to set up chairs or risers or equipment when needed? Are you gracious to your family, lay people, or visitors on Sunday mornings at church? People are watching us all of the time. Demonstrate servant leadership as you do your daily tasks at church with your people.

I am often reminded when working with those in my care that Jesus is the chief shepherd. This ministry that I am privileged to steward at my church is actually Jesus' ministry. This church that I serve is not my church but Jesus' church. Jesus died for his church. We show our love for Jesus by the way we care for his church.

What are some practical ways worship ministers can love their people? We love our people by:

1. being more concerned about their souls than the music,
2. taking time to get to know those in our ministry,
3. praying for those in our ministry,
4. checking on those in our ministry who are having a difficult time,
5. investing in our people to help them to grow as disciples, and
6. making ourself available by arriving early and staying late at rehearsals and services in order to speak to people.

A number of years ago my worship team was preparing a fairly involved musical drama for Easter. One week before the first presentation, one of the lead actors in the musical pulled me aside before a rehearsal. He quietly told me he had just gotten word that his father, who lived several states away, had suffered a sudden heart and died. Obviously, this young man was hurting and would be leaving immediately to travel home. My first thought as the young man shared this tragic news was all about the Easter musical. What would I do to replace this person since he would be a distance away at his father's funeral? Fortunately, I did not express this thought to the young man. Later I felt strongly convicted that I was more concerned about the musical than I was for this young man who had lost his father. The program had become more important than the people. The Lord used this situation to help me see that my priorities were way off balance. This musical presentation should never be more important than the people who are serving in the worship ministry.

How well are we loving the people in our ministries week in and week out? Are we more focused on the structures of the ministry than the people? Ministry is messy because it is made up of people just like us who are sinners saved by the grace of our great Lord. One of the most challenging aspects of worship ministry is loving your congregation and your worship teams.

Lord, grow us in this area of loving people. Help us shepherd your people in such a way that is pleasing to you. Amen.

CHAPTER 9

The Worship Minister's Family

Husbands, love your wives, as Christ loved the church and gave himself up for her.
Ephesians 5:25

Fathers, do not provoke your children to anger, but bring them up in the discipline and instruction of the Lord.
Ephesians 6:4

He must manage his household well, with all dignity keeping his children submissive, for if someone does not know how to manage his own household, how will he care for God's church?
1 Timothy 3:4–5

These are challenging days for Christian families. I believe it is especially challenging for ministers and their families. Because I did not grow up in a minister's home, I really did not know what that would be like until I was in ministry and married with children. The worship minister needs to see his family as the first place of ministry. Our families need to know that they are our first priority over the ministry work at the church.

Balancing work hours in ministry with time at home is an ongoing task. The minister often feels overwhelmed with ministry needs and the time it takes to meet those needs. Ministry needs seem unending and can quickly overwhelm the minister's schedule and family life. In the worship minister's month-to-month schedule there are usually seasons of ebb and flow. The Christmas and Easter seasons and the time leading up to these special days can be challenging to our schedules. Other times of the year can be busy as well depending on scheduled church events that occur. Our families can more easily accept these busy times when we are away extra hours if we are careful other seasons of the year to find additional time for family needs. We must always be on guard so that our ministries do not cause us to neglect our families.

When thinking about making family a priority, our spouse should be top priority. The relationship of the husband and wife in ministry settings sets the tone for a healthy family life and demonstrates to the church a picture of a strong Christian marriage. Because worship ministers have seasons of busier ministry schedules, the spouse is often left managing the family needs alone. Worship ministers are never excused from family responsibilities just because they serve in ministry. Except for those times when emergency situations arise that call for a minister to be present in a church member's crisis, ministers need to organize their schedules to be home at reasonable times and stay firm with the schedule. If your family is expecting you home by 6:00 p.m., make that happen on a consistent basis.

The role of the minister's spouse is a calling that is quite challenging. For young worship ministers planning for marriage, there needs to be intentional conversations with your future spouse about being a minister's spouse. This topic should be explored early in marriage counseling sessions. If your future spouse is not sure about this role or not called to this role, take more time before the marriage for prayer and consideration. At some point, if this is not resolved you may need to rethink your plans for ministry or marriage.

Even though the minister's wife is not on the church staff, she is a key person to the success of the worship minister and his ministry. Her support, encouragement, assistance, wisdom, and prayers bring great strength to the worship minister and his work. Churches need to understand that when they call the worship minister they are not also hiring his wife. The minister's spouse needs to be involved at the church just as any other dedicated lay person would be, yet without expectations that she will take on some large leadership role. When the minister's children are young sometimes all the spouse can do is take care of the children's needs because her husband is in a demanding ministry position. Taking on challenging leadership roles at the church may be too much in these years. As the children get older the spouse can consider taking on a larger role at the church. In whatever role the spouse accepts at the church, there should always be evidence of her love for the church and support for the pastor and staff.

Church members will sometimes seek the opinion of a minister's spouse on current issues at the church. In these situations it is important that the spouse show support for the church leadership. It is best to not vocalize thoughts that could be seen in opposition to the direction of the church leadership or pastor. The role of the minister's spouse can be a tightrope walk at times. A minister's wife who is too vocal on a church issue or conflict can cause great damage to her husband and his leadership at the church. As discussed earlier, a worship minister should not speak out in conflict with the pastor or other church staff. This rule applies to the minister's spouse as well.

Worship ministers need to be in control of their calendar so time is reserved for family. He should plan time on the calendar for date nights with his spouse. If this is not done in advance it is very likely a church event will be scheduled on one of the evenings. Granted, sometimes you may need to reschedule a date night depending on what the church activity may be; however, if you are not intentional about putting this on your calendar something else will take its place. Making sure you clearly communicate your daily and weekly schedule with your spouse can help with planning especially when you have children. Thinking of ways to relieve your spouse from being the chief caregiver for your children gives her a break from the daily routine. Being in touch with your spouse throughout the workday by phone or messaging keeps lines of communication open.

My wife was such a great encouragement to me when I was in full-time worship ministry over the years. When the Lord blessed us with children, she was a wonderful mother. I remember the many years when I would leave early for church services on Sunday and she would be responsible for getting the children out of bed, dressed, fed, and transported to church. She played such a sacrificial role in order to help me do worship ministry. She was (and still is) my partner in the ministry.

Ministry is difficult because it is not an 8-to-5 job. The hours vary and the job never seems to be finished. There is not much closure to the work of the ministry. It is an ongoing process. The challenge for the minister when arriving home in the evening is to turn off what has been happening in the day and focus on his wife and family. Often times, when the minister is at home he is not really at home due to interruptions from phone calls, messaging, and email. One minister shared with me that he puts his cell phone in the bedroom when he gets home and leaves it there.

Another challenge when the minister arrives home is to not unload on his spouse all of the stressful, sometimes negative things that happened during the day while serving the church. It is not unusual to have conflict issues with other church staff members, the pastor, or lay people that need to be settled. One of my goals was not to share these things in such a way that my wife would become bitter or even angry towards the pastor, staff, or church members. I do not think I was always successful at doing this. The worship minister should wait to share some things until he has time to pray and sort through his own thoughts and feelings on a matter. Often when we share right after an event occurs we say things we do not really mean. After we work through our thoughts on the matter we would probably relay the situation to our spouse differently. It is possible that your spouse can become even more angry or bitter about these matters than you are as the minister. She could see these incidents as attacks on her husband and grow defensive. I am not advocating for the minister to withhold information from his wife but advising that he express himself in such a way that shows love toward the others who are involved. My goal over the many years of ministry was that my wife's love for the church would not diminish but grow.

When children enter the picture, the minister's family becomes more complicated. It may seem that the minister's family is like living in a fishbowl because everyone is watching intently to see how things are going. Members of the church know which children are the minister's children and can have a higher level of expectation for the minister's children than they do for other children in the church. Sometimes as a worship minister I found myself being more concerned about what church members thought about my children than I was about the needs of my children. The needs of your children always outweigh your concern for what the perception of church members may be towards your children.

Children are sinners just like everyone else in the church. There will be times when they do something openly that may embarrass their parents just like all children sometimes do. As children move into their teen or young adult years these types of events can take on more serious implications. Ministers' families are not immune from having a straying child. As parents we need to lovingly work through these times with our children, praying for wisdom. Love your child the way the Heavenly Father loves you by showing mercy and grace. A loving church will be supportive to the minister's family in difficult times like these.

Children have a lot of pressure these days to perform well in school, excel in athletics, and succeed in music activities. As I look back on my children growing up and leaving home as young adults, the most important goal I had for them (and still do) is that they would walk with Jesus and mature in their relationship with him. All of the other goals tend to work out if this primary goal is achieved. This may sound simplistic, but often parents are so focused on their son or daughter being successful in life that they miss the most important priority—their child's relationship to Christ.

Should a minister's children participate in every church activity? We do desire that they be involved in the life of the church. As a child ages the level of participation often becomes more. The church cannot be the substitute for the spiritual training that should be ongoing in the home, but the church can certainly come alongside the minister's family in this area. My children had wonderful Christian men and women working with them throughout their growing-up years in the church. These teachers and leaders made a great impact on my children. I am especially grateful for student ministers who spent time with my children during their teen years, modeling the Christian life, teaching the Scriptures, and taking them on mission trips. Your children do not have to do every church activity, but as a parent I wanted my children to take advantage of as many of these spiritual opportunities as possible. I desired for my children to hear the gospel at home and church.

As your children mature their activities outside the home increase. They are frequently involved in sport teams or music groups. My children played baseball, soccer, basketball, ran on the track team, sang in choirs, played in school bands, and more. One of my goals at the beginning of a season was to be present as much as I could at all of their events. I remember many Saturday mornings sitting out at a soccer field in cold, damp air as my children played. There were many evenings watching high school football games and Saturday band competitions. These events were on my calendar along with everything else I was doing. I wanted to make my children's activities a top priority in my schedule. Showing love and care to your children is not just about quality time; it is also quantity time. If the worship minister fails to get these dates on the calendar early, other events crowd them out.

When my children were in their preschool years I thought I had all the time in the world to spend with them. As I look back on those years, they went by very fast. Children grow up, leave home, get married, and have careers. Though it may seem your elementary-age child will always be around home, one day the house will be quiet and you will wonder where all the time went. If not careful, worship ministers can let these years go by because they are so busy in ministry. They fail to see their children grow up.

The minister's spouse and family are the first place of ministry. Prioritizing your time and attention to your family is crucial to the health of your family and your ministry. If you lose your family, you lose your ministry.

CHAPTER 10

Organizing Your Week—Time Management in Worship Ministry

A NUMBER OF YEARS ago I had a conversation with a lay person that wondered how a worship minister could work full-time hours. What does the worship minister do besides lead worship on Sundays and rehearse the worship teams on Wednesday night? What people see on Sundays and Wednesdays is perhaps the most visible part of the worship minister's work. What worship ministers do during the weekdays is the foundational portion of that ministry.

Serving in a full-time worship ministry often feels like being self-employed. Self-employed people determine how to spend their time each day in order to keep their business moving forward. Although worship ministry is not a business, there are a number of things that must take place every week in order to ensure a healthy worship ministry at your church. The worship minister's schedule during the week can be fairly open ended. Most of the time there is no one supervising you and ordering your day. Each new day is a day the worship minister seeks to be a good steward of his time and the resources the church places at his disposal.

Time management for the worship minister requires a great deal of self-discipline. Except for scheduled meetings and appointments, you are determining your daily schedule. How will you efficiently use your time? Are you able to stay on task and focus on the things that should be accomplished? The ministry is not a place for lazy people. Your church may not know all that you do in your weekly work, but they do know if you are organized and prepared to lead when the church is gathered.

Section II: Leading the Worship Ministry

What are some of the possible weekly activities of a worship minister?

- Staff meetings
- Meetings with your pastor
- Other meetings
- Lunch meetings
- Calendar planning
- Worship service planning
- Scheduling instrumentalists, singers, tech team for upcoming services
- Rehearsal planning for choirs and worship teams
- Counseling
- Mentoring
- Setting up for rehearsals
- Communicating with team members, other church members
- Preparing to lead rehearsals
- Coordinating music groups that others lead (children's choirs, other worship bands)
- Personal preparation to lead worship services (practicing songs, working on transitions)
- Hospital visits
- Outreach visits for church
- Preparing Bible studies for small groups you may lead
- Leading rehearsals (choir, worship band, other groups)
- Spiritual development (time for you to stay refreshed in God's Word)
- Song discovery
- Leading your tech team
- Keeping tech equipment and instruments in working order
- Long range planning for the worship ministry
- Writing assignments such as blog-type articles
- Supervising assistants or interns in worship ministry

Organizing Your Week—Time Management in Worship Ministry

- Assisting with church events that are not necessarily worship ministry related
- Discovering new worship team singers, instrumentalists
- Completing other tasks assigned by your pastor

Each weekday in worship ministry can be full of tasks to accomplish as well as meetings both formal and informal. Sometimes how you plan a day is not at all how the day turns out to be. Flexibility is important on those days when something takes more time than you planned.

Because no one really hands you a daily schedule of things to accomplish, the worship minister must seek to bring some organization to each day. After serving in full-time worship ministry for a while, I have discovered that setting a regular schedule for each day of the week is helpful. There are certain tasks that you know need to be accomplished on particular days. Having a daily routine of tasks to accomplish gives you a starting point for each day. I have found that if I am not disciplined about accomplishing certain tasks during the first part of the week, it is possible to get to the end of the week and have too many duties to perform. At that point you are working into the weekend.

Here is a typical week in my worship ministry schedule:

Monday—staff meeting(s), begin worship planning for next Sunday, work on any issues from the previous Sunday (correspondence with team members, evaluating the worship service, equipment or instrument issues), communicate with your worship teams about the next Sunday, outreach to visitors from Sunday

Tuesday—hospital visitation (could take half the day), finalize worship planning for Sunday

Wednesday—preparation for evening rehearsals, readying rehearsal areas so when teams arrive everything is in order to begin the rehearsal, preparing for choir practice, church dinner, prayer meeting/worship time and rehearsals during the evening

Thursday—deal with any issues from Wednesday night rehearsals, clean up, spend time in worship preparation for Sunday

Friday—usually a day off unless something is planned at church

Saturday—usually a day off unless something is planned at church

Sunday—full day of worship services and rehearsals

Obviously, some of these days would be different for other worship ministers. The main point is to have a daily plan of how you will steward your time where you serve. I want my church to know that I'm bringing a high quality of service to the worship ministry each week.

Worship ministers should settle on a daily schedule and let others know that schedule. Your pastor needs to be familiar with your work schedule as well as the office staff. Set a normal time you will come into the office and when you will leave. You should arrive fairly early when the office is open. Your church may require you to keep certain office hours or they may be open to a more flexible schedule. Since ministers often work in the evenings and on weekends, it is common for them to be in the office only at certain times of the day.

The office staff needs to know your schedule. They are the ones answering the phone and assisting church members who may want to meet with you. The office staff should always know where you are during office hours. Do not keep them guessing as to what your schedule is. If you are going to be arriving late one morning, alert someone in the office to this. If you are in a lunch meeting, let them know when you will arrive back at the office. If you are spending the day in study at home, notify them of your plans. Show accountability with your time and schedule. It can be quite frustrating to the office staff when they constantly try to determine where staff members are or when they will be in the office.

On most days you will have unexpected interruptions. Often these interruptions are from church members or staff who drop by your office to talk. During these times of interruptions you need to have the sensitivity to know if this is a quick conversation or a more involved discussion. At these points pray for the Lord's wisdom to know if you need to alter your schedule or simply greet the person for a moment and then get back to work. I do believe that the Lord puts people in our path each day and we need to have the sensitivity to know when we need to take some time to minister, counsel, or even pray with them.

In addition to having a daily routine for your work, it is helpful to keep a "to do" list. I served with a staff member who kept a 3x5 card in his shirt pocket with his "to do" list. It was always close by and he would be adding to the list throughout the day as he was talking with people. Today there are other ways to keep an up to date "to do" list such as an app on your phone or laptop. I use the "to do" list app on my phone to keep track of projects that need my focus. I add to the list and check the list to remind myself

Organizing Your Week—Time Management in Worship Ministry

what needs to be accomplished. Occasionally, I will find an extra twenty or thirty minutes in my schedule when I've completed one task or meeting. At these points I look at my list to see what else I could complete in that short amount of time. Every person has the same amount of hours in the day. The stewardship of this time is your challenge.

Consider keeping a list of big ideas or dreams for your ministry (discussed in the next chapter). What would you like to see accomplished next year or in five years? Make a list of these ideas. Pray about them to discern the Lord's leadership on this. Consider how to make this future plan work.

If you do not have a daily plan for your week and a "to do" list, you will find yourself wasting time and accomplishing little for the kingdom. The Apostle Paul told us to "look carefully then how you walk, not as unwise but as wise, making the best use of the time, because the days are evil" (Eph 5:15–16). Remember that two of the character traits listed for elders in the church are self-control and discipline (Titus 1:8). As worship ministers we want to be good stewards of the time the Lord has given us. We are serving a great God and a congregation that is looking to us for leadership. How we plan our days and use the time we have been allotted for kingdom work has eternal impact.

CHAPTER 11

Planning the Worship Ministry Calendar

THE OLD SAYING "FAILING to plan is planning to fail" still applies to those serving in worship ministry. Without serious thoughtful planning it is possible to go through years of ministry and seem like not much has been accomplished. Every worship minister should have a five-year plan and a yearly plan for the worship ministry. Your philosophy of worship ministry (see chapter 3) guides these plans. What are the main purposes of the worship ministry in the local church? These purposes are implemented through thoughtful long-range planning and yearly planning.

As you begin a worship ministry position, spending time in prayer seeking the Lord's guidance for this new ministry is a top priority. Talking with your pastor and church leadership about their expectations and dreams for the worship ministry can also give you direction for several years of planning. Your worship ministry dreams are accomplished when you have a map that shows you a way forward. This map is your five-year worship ministry plan.

Once you have a five-year plan, work backwards to see the steps you need to take in order to reach the intended goals in the plan. Put these steps onto your calendar. For many of these goals you will need the church to appropriate the budget resources to reach the goals. This can take some time since most churches are working on budget planning a year or two in advance.

What are some goals a worship minister might list on a five-year plan?

- Transitioning the worship style of the church

Planning the Worship Ministry Calendar

- Expanding the number of church members involved in worship ministry
- Enriching discipleship opportunities to members of the worship team
- Beginning a children's choir ministry
- Beginning a student worship band or choir ministry
- Recruiting and training new tech team members
- Beginning a new music academy to teach music skills to church members
- Planning mission outreach opportunities for the church worship teams (local and international missions)
- Planning and developing special evenings of worship (seasonal services, special worship nights)
- Updating the sound system in the worship center
- Updating the projector system/screens in the worship center
- Redesigning the platform area of the worship center to accommodate more current needs of the worship teams

Obviously, many of these goals could be accomplished within a particular year, but you would not want to attempt to do very many of these at one time. This is why a five-year plan gives direction to your ministry. What should be the top priority goals? What do you sense from the Lord in your prayer times concerning these goals? What does your pastor think are the main goals that need immediate attention?

Another consideration to setting goals that will make major changes in the worship ministry is how soon to act on these goals. Unless there is some sense of great urgency or the leadership of your church is insisting on making some immediate changes, it is probably best to not make major changes in your worship ministry early in your tenure at the church. One of the most important roles for you as worship minister when you arrive at a new place of service is to observe and build relationships. The worship minister must learn the culture of the church and community. Sometimes your five-year plan needs to slow down a little in order for you to give time for the people to build trust in your leadership.

How long does it take a congregation to trust you and your plans for the worship ministry? Some of that may depend on the location of your church. Are you in an urban, suburban, or rural area? Sometimes churches

Section II: Leading the Worship Ministry

located in smaller towns or rural areas take longer to build trust in their minister's leadership. Former pastors and staff members who may have caused distrust among the church leadership can also influence a congregation's trust in the current pastor and staff. Another problem with building relationships and trust is that pastors and staff often leave the church at the very time relationships are maturing. Pastors and staff members who have long tenures are usually able to influence change and reach goals quicker. They have loved and served their congregations for a longer period of time and their people trust them.

As you begin working towards your goals, continue adding new goals to your long-range plan for future dreams. Your long-range plan is never really finished. This keeps you moving forward in ministry at your church.

Yearly planning includes your long-range goals and recurring ministry activities. Usually in early June, I work on a worship ministry calendar for the upcoming year. This calendar begins in August and runs through the next summer. It is important to put all major worship ministry events on this calendar. After determining particular dates I would then make sure these dates are included on the main church calendar and that rooms are reserved for these events. Of course major worship events need to be approved by your pastor. You also want to ensure the event fits well on the church calendar so that it does not conflict or give competition to another major church event.

These are the types of events that you need to include on your yearly worship ministry calendar:

- Seasonal worship musicals/services such as Christmas programs, Christmas Eve services, Easter services
- Other worship ministry events such as special worship nights
- Children's choir music programs
- Worship team fellowships
- Worship team extra rehearsals
- Worship team retreats
- Additional choir rehearsals for seasonal services
- Training events
- Worship ministry missions events
- Choir rehearsal start-up dates

Planning the Worship Ministry Calendar

- Audition times for worship ministry teams
- Other concerts
- Mission trips

You may serve in a church that expects you to present musical services for Christmas and Easter. These types of events require a great amount of advanced planning. They also require extra rehearsals and other work to physically set up the platform. These times must be reserved on the church calendar in advance. A good amount of coordination goes into planning a musical event such as this.

A number of years ago I recall a calendar conflict concerning our annual Christmas worship musical. Somehow a wedding was scheduled on Saturday the same weekend as our musical. Although the worship musical would normally happen on Sunday, we would not have access to the worship center for stage preparation and a dress rehearsal. That particular year I failed to reserve the worship center for the week before our program. It was reserved on Sunday but not the days that led up to Sunday. This was my oversight and did not happen in the following years. That year we decided to move our musical to the next weekend.

How well the worship ministry functions depends greatly on your planning skills as a worship minister. Working on a five-year plan and a yearly plan is crucial to accomplishing worship ministry goals. When you place your worship ministry plans on a calendar and begin working towards accomplishing your plans, you help the church staff and lay people to include the worship ministry in their plans.

CHAPTER 12

The Worship Pastor's Resources (Budgeting)

Often when churches want to move from a part-time to a full-time worship ministry position they look for extra funds in their budget to pull together enough support for this new worship ministry position. What they sometimes fail to consider is that in addition to providing for the worship minister's income this person will also need resources in order to do the work of the ministry at that local church. These resources might include sound equipment, music purchases, instruments, and a number of other needs. Sometimes there may not be much left to supply these resources and the worship minister has to be creative or go without these things. When talking to a church about a ministry position at some point it would be helpful to know if the church allowed for a worship ministry budget. It is also helpful to know what they already have in the way of instruments and equipment to help with the worship ministry.

Most churches operate with an annual budget that projects spending in the many areas of the church's ministry. Budgets include such things as salaries and benefits for ministers and staff, utilities, insurance, maintenance of the church buildings, debt retirement, replacement of equipment, emergency contingency funds, and missions support. In this budget planning there are also expenditure plans for ministries of the church such as small group Bible study materials, children's ministry needs, student ministry, and worship ministry.

There is a financial team and treasurer nominated by the church to oversee the church budget, budget planning, and expenditures. The

The Worship Pastor's Resources (Budgeting)

worship minister usually is asked to submit a proposed budget for the new fiscal year that details needs and desires for expenditures in the worship ministry. What are some expense items that should be listed in the worship ministry budget?

- New music for worship services
- New music for the choir
- Music and resources for children's' choirs
- Subscriptions to online worship planning tools such as CCLI (copyright license), Songselect, Praisecharts, Planning Center
- Piano tuning expenses
- Instrument equipment maintenance
- Sound equipment maintenance
- Worship ministry training events
- Special seasonal musical programs (Christmas, Easter)
- Worship ministry fellowship events
- New sound equipment purchases
- New music equipment purchases
- Supplies (batteries, miscellaneous needs)
- Worship ministry mission trips (children, students, adults)

Considering what worship resources will be needed for the next year requires prayer and careful attention to the church's overall goals for the new year. You are a steward of the worship ministry budget. You will be spending money that has been given to the church by its members in order to carry out the work of ministry. With that in mind, the worship minister needs to be serious about the use of the resources available in the worship ministry budget.

When putting together a worship ministry budget for a financial team to view, it is best to itemize all expected expenses. Giving the team one yearly amount for the worship ministry budget without careful itemization is not helpful and almost always guarantees you will not get the amount you requested for your budget. Here is a sample worship ministry budget.

SECTION II: LEADING THE WORSHIP MINISTRY

COMMUNITY CHURCH PROPOSED WORSHIP MINISTRY BUDGET

New Music for Worship	**$3660.00**
12 new worship songs (chord charts, lead sheets) @ $30 per song	360.00
20 new choir anthems (50 copies @ $2 per anthem)	2000.00
Christmas music for choir (50 copies @ $8 per book)	400.00
Orchestration for choir Christmas music	600.00
Easter music for choir (3 anthems, 50 copies each @ $2)	300.00
Children's Choirs	**$1800.00**
Quarterly curriculum resource packets and music (3 quarters @ $200)	600.00
Fellowship activities (3 events @ $100 per event)	300.00
Training for children's choir leaders (retreat and media resources)	400.00
Summer music camp at church (music day camp for children)	500.00
Miscellaneous Expenses	**$1620.00**
Planning Center Online (worship planning tool @ $60 per month)	720.00
Guest musicians for special events	500.00
CCLI license (copyright license to project and print texts)	400.00
Worship Team Discipleship	**$1820.00**
Study books (2 books for 20 team members @ $8 per book)	320.00
Fellowships for worship ministry teams	500.00
Training events—guest speakers, retreats	1000.00
Music Instrument Needs	**$4750.00**
Repair of amps or instruments	500.00
Replace bass amp	750.00
Purchase new keyboard	2500.00
Piano tunings (10 tunings for 3 pianos @ $100 per tuning)	1000.00
Sound and Lighting Equipment Needs	**$3990.00**
3 new wireless microphones @ $500	1500.00
12 new microphone and instrument cables @ $20	240.00
3 new direct boxes @ $100	300.00
Batteries for wireless microphones (25 9-volt batteries per month @ $2 per battery)	600.00
Equipment repair	750.00

Replace data projector bulbs (2 @300 per bulb)	600.00
Total Proposed Worship Ministry Budget	$17640.00

Other items to consider for the budget depend on the particular worship ministry needs of your church. If the worship ministry is more traditional, then you would need to include such items as organ maintenance and tuning (pipe organ), choir robe cleaning, handbell and orchestra music, music program printing for special events, and music storage boxes for choir music and choir folders. Sometimes the financial team may put any new equipment purchases in one location in the budget or repair expenses in one location. This would give a better "big picture" view of these expenses.

If you increase the amount of the worship ministry budget from the previous year, you need to give a rationale for the additional requests in the worship ministry budget. Help your financial team understand why you need the additional resources.

PRINCIPLES TO CONSIDER WHEN PREPARING WORSHIP MINISTRY BUDGETS

1. Spend time in prayer seeking the Lord's guidance concerning next year's plans for the worship ministry. Use this plan to guide your budgeting process.
2. Look at your five-year goals and decide how to budget for those goals as the time approaches to enact the goals.
3. Be considerate of other ministry leaders and their needs at your church. The worship ministry is not the only area that needs resources.
4. Be realistic with the figures you put in your budget. Don't overinflate amounts to insure you receive what you think are your needs. Be honest and forthcoming about the budget amounts.
5. Know that you may not receive what you perceive are crucial budget needs and have the right Christ-like attitude with your financial team.
6. Remember you are a steward of the Lord's money. Approach the use of your budget money for worship ministry as a sacred trust.

Section II: Leading the Worship Ministry

7. Remember the Lord will supply every need of yours according to his riches in glory in Christ Jesus (Phil 4:19).
8. Keep in mind that God's work done in God's way will never lack God's provision (Hudson Taylor).

At one church where I served I followed a worship minister who had served the church for over fifteen years. He was well loved and did a great job leading the worship ministry at the church. I stepped into a well-established worship ministry with good resources already in place. It took several years before I felt that the worship ministry reflected more of my leadership than my predecessor. I was reminded of the stewardship of this worship ministry and the legacy left behind by the former minister. I reflected on the people who served in that worship ministry over the years. I also thought about the fine musical and technical equipment that was available.

In Deuteronomy 6:10–15 the Lord reminds the children of Israel that when they come into the promised land they will inherit great cities they did not build, houses full of good things that they did not fill, cisterns that they did not dig, and vineyards and olive trees they did not plant. The challenge before the children of Israel when they did receive these gifts was to remember that the Lord gave them these many blessings and so to be grateful and good stewards.

Those of us in the ministry are stewards of the resources we inherit and those we acquire as time moves forward. Our gracious Lord supplies these resources. We need to be grateful and intentional about using them to his glory and not forget his loving kindness toward us. As you think about the resources of your worship ministry, remember to keep the focus on the Lord and the kingdom ministry he allows you and me to steward.

One day your ministry at a particular church will come to close and you will leave that worship ministry to another leader who will use the resources you have stewarded. What will you leave behind? I hope you will leave behind a worship ministry with great resources—not just physical things but also trained lay leaders who love Jesus that will help the new leader carry on where you left off.

CHAPTER 13

Hospital Ministry

MINISTERING TO YOUR WORSHIP team members goes beyond the times you are in rehearsals and worship services. It is the weekly care that the worship minister provides outside the church building that makes a great impact with your worship team members for the kingdom. It seems there is always some crisis happening in a member's family such as issues with aging parents, personal health problems, or concerns with children. In these situations it is not a matter of knowing *whether* you should respond but rather *how* you should respond. Often in these crisis situations you will need to visit a church member in the hospital. Your pastor may carry the load of the regular hospital ministry, but you as the worship minister still have a responsibility to check on worship team members and their families when they are in the hospital.

Many multi-staff churches assign particular days of the week for their ministers to make hospital visits. For the worship minister you may have one day each week you are expected to check on members in the hospital. If your church is in a more urban setting, you could spend half of your day or more making these visits because church members could be spread out across the city in different hospitals. I am grateful that early in my ministry I had a pastor who took me along on his hospital visits and showed me what to do. If you have not been in a hospital setting much, it can be a little overwhelming at first. Consider these suggestions to help you be effective in hospital ministry.

If your church expects you to visit the hospital on a particular day of the week, usually your church receptionist or administrative assistant will help compile a list of members who are in the hospital. You need to know the hospital and room number for each church member. As you plan to go, dress professionally. If you dress fairly casually at the church office during the week, on the day you make hospital visits dress a little more formally. If you have a nametag, put this on as you make your visits. This alerts the hospital professional staff of your role. Consider taking a Bible along on your visits. Even though we now have Scripture on mobile devices, it is beneficial for the church members to see you using a Bible (especially the older church members).

As you visit a church member at the hospital, remember that you do not need to stay very long. The person may be tired or find it difficult to be social for an extended period of time. In addition you will probably have several other members to visit and need to limit interaction in order to see all on your list. If the person appears to be sleeping, knock lightly on the door to see if he will respond. You can come back again later if necessary. Leave a business card with a personal note on the back of the card near the patient's bed so he will know you came to check on him.

When talking with the church member, do not ask for details concerning the illness, procedure, or surgery. Let the person volunteer the information. It is always best not to tell stories of someone else who had the same health situation, especially if that other person did not do well. Years ago I had knee surgery due to an injury. Several well-meaning people told me the difficulties their friends or family experienced with knee surgery. One person told me that I would never run again (thankfully that was not the case). We need to remember that we are at the hospital to encourage our church members. Only the Lord knows the outcome of the situation and in him all things are possible.

As you enter the room, introduce yourself and tell them you are from the church. Sometimes church members will remember the senior pastor but have not had the chance to meet you. After you greet one another, ask how things are going. Ask how you can pray for him and his family. Consider if there is an appropriate Scripture passage to read. Sometimes when the patient is facing difficult decisions about their health situation, reading a Psalm or another passage can help to remind them of the Lord's care for him. At this point take a few moments to pray for the church member. If there are other family members or friends in the room, include them in the prayer time. After praying let the member know you will relay information to your pastor and that the church will continue to check on him.

Hospital Ministry

Occasionally before you enter a patient's room you may see a sign on the door that tells you to wash your hands or to wear a mask before entering. This is not to protect you from getting what the patient has but to protect the patient whose immune system is very low. If the patient were truly contagious, you would not be allowed in the room. You may also find a doctor or nurse working with a patient as you enter the room. It is best in these situations to come back by that room fifteen minutes later and wait until the procedure or consultation is over. Often a patient will be away from the room for a procedure. When this occurs be sure to leave your business card with a note stating that you are praying for him.

You may discover that your church member is in an intensive care unit with restricted visitation. In this situation first go to the nurses' station, and introduce yourself, stating that you are a minister from the patient's church. Ask if it is possible to visit the patient. The nurse will usually tell you how the patient is doing and if he is able to have a visitor. Often in the intensive care unit you will find that the church member is not conscious or is sleeping. Most intensive care units have special waiting room areas for family members. After checking on the church member go by the waiting room area to see if any family members are present. When a church member is in intensive care, the family members who are waiting should get your focus. If you go to a waiting area and do not know who the family members are, ask if there is anyone present who is related to the church member. If they happen to be present, find out what the family's needs are and how you can pray for them. Take a few moments to pray with the family.

As you visit in the hospital remember that you may be the only visitor the church member will have that will speak about spiritual things. You probably cannot help with the person's physical needs, which may seem looming at the time, but you can certainly bring a gospel perspective to the situation. We should not just be focused on the physical situation but the spiritual condition of the person. Church members in the hospital are sometimes facing life-and-death situations and need to be reminded about their security in Christ.

If you know of a worship team member that is having a procedure or surgery, make a special effort to go by the hospital or outpatient facility on the day of the surgery. Arrive early so you can spend a few minutes praying with the church member and conversing with the family prior to the surgery. You do not need to stay for the whole procedure but being there at the beginning to pray can be very important to your worship team member.

Section II: Leading the Worship Ministry

After you complete your visits be sure to give your pastor an update on each visit. He needs to be informed. If you cannot see your pastor right away, take a few moments to send him an email update on each patient.

I recall one of the most intense hospital visits I have made. It was about 2:00am one morning when I received a call from one of my young worship team members asking me to come to the hospital because his wife had just passed away. She had terminal cancer for a number of months and that night was rushed to the hospital. My immediate thought upon receiving the call was that I would not know what to say to this worship team member when I arrived. Even though his wife's death was expected the news was still devastating. My prayer as I traveled to the hospital was for the Lord to give me words of wisdom. When I arrived at the hospital room, I saw my worship team member and other family members sobbing. My first reaction was to hug my team member and cry with him. I then led in a prayer for the family and stayed with them for a while. In these situations your presence is especially important even when you do not have words to say. Reading Scripture at times like these is better than any words you may think to say.

In one church I served my hospital day was Tuesday. When Tuesdays came around each week, I usually felt stressed to get a number of things accomplished in the office and did not always have a good attitude about dropping everything to go to the hospital. After I would finish my hospital visits, I was always reminded that this kind of ministry is more important than office work at my desk. Visiting the hospital may seem daunting at first, but you should not be afraid to go and encourage your church members. The Lord will guide you each step of the way. Even though you go to minister to them, it is often you who receives the greatest blessing.

CHAPTER 14

Dealing with Conflicts

YOU HAVE PROBABLY HEARD the saying, "Ministry would be easy if it weren't for the people." This is an amusing thought since ministry is all about people. Sometimes there will be church members that seem difficult. You may think their main purpose in life is to see how frustrated they can make you. I had three church members in my first full-time ministry setting that I thought were difficult. It could have been their strong personalities or perhaps they did not trust me as a young minister. Upon leaving that church for a new place of service I left these church members for someone else to enjoy. However, it did not take me long to discover that those same difficult people were in my new church but they had different names. No matter where you serve you will find church members who are challenging. There are times when you need to work through conflicts. Let me encourage you to approach these times with much prayer and to work through the conflicts rather than ignoring the problem.

One of the most helpful passages when thinking about conflict is James 1:19–20: "Know this, my beloved brothers: let every person be quick to hear, slow to speak, slow to anger; for the anger of man does not produce the righteousness of God." In this passage the emphasis is on listening and not responding at the same emotional level that the person speaking to you may have. Ephesians 4:26 is another helpful passage: "Be angry and do not sin; do not let the sun go down on your anger." Here we see the importance of dealing with conflict sooner rather than later. In fact, if possible one should deal with conflict on the same day of the occurrence.

Section II: Leading the Worship Ministry

It seems that when a conflict arises for the worship minister it often happens before or after a worship service. These are times when you are least able to work through an issue. When a conflict happens you may also be extremely tired, such as after a rehearsal. This can be the worst possible time for you to try and respond. You will find that you may say something you will regret, something you would not say when you are rested.

Here are some practical suggestions in dealing with conflict in your ministry setting.

1. When someone wants to discuss a situation with you, do not try to respond if you are tired or in a rush. Take a few minutes to listen to the church member. Let the person know that you value his/her opinion. Ask if you can talk at a later time so you have an opportunity to consider the things that were said and then decide a time to meet. By doing this you will have time to rest, pray, consult with your pastor, and handle the conflict in a more Christ-like way.

2. When you are listening to a church member who is unhappy with the way you have done something, do not be defensive. Do not rush to give an answer supporting your action. Often times in these situations I find that I do not listen well because I am formulating a response as the person is sharing. Approach these situations with great humility. Remind yourself that you are not perfect and that you will make mistakes sometimes.

3. If the church member is emotionally upset when explaining the conflict, remember that no explanation you make will satisfy the situation. The person is not in a good frame of mind to listen to your explanation. Discussing this at a later time when emotions have cooled down will help to get this conflict solved.

4. Do not allow yourself to respond on the same emotional level as the person who is speaking to you. Stay calm (slow to speak, slow to anger). "A soft answer turns away wrath, but a harsh word stirs up anger" (Prov 15:1). Respond back with clarifying questions such as, "This is what I hear you saying ... Is that correct?" This will help to ensure you understand what the person is saying.

5. If you schedule another time to talk about the issue, it may be wise to include a third person that can listen to both sides of the conflict. This

also provides you some accountability concerning what is said or not said.

6. Remember there is usually at least a kernel of truth in every conflict situation. Consider if there is something you need to change in your worship ministry to alleviate the problem. What can you learn from this interaction?

7. If you are regularly dealing with conflict in your ministry from people that are normally agreeable, perhaps the problem is you. Are you leading your worship ministry in such a way that causes conflict? Perhaps it is time to sit down with your pastor or a counselor to discuss possible weaknesses in your leadership style.

As a worship minister you will also find yourself in situations where you need to speak a difficult word to a worship team member. Perhaps you need to ask a worship team member to take a break from the worship ministry or to not serve in the ministry. This could be for a number of reasons, including the person's lifestyle decisions, family issues, and dependability. These kinds of conversations should not be delayed because you want to avoid an unpleasant situation.

Here are some suggestions in dealing with these types of conflicts.

1. If the issue has been an ongoing problem for sometime, it is best to discuss this with the team member in a timely way. Document when you talked with the team member about the problem. Look to see if the team member works to correct the problem over a period of time.

2. After having several conversations with the team member and the problem is not being corrected, it is best for the team member to leave the team. At this point talk to your pastor about the situation. Make sure you both agree on this decision before you take action.

3. When you meet with the worship team member, have a third person present for accountability.

4. Explain your decision and give time for the team member to respond.

5. Work towards a redemptive solution.

6. If the issue has to do with a moral failure or some other serious situation, the worship team member should be removed immediately, keeping in mind Galatians 6:1–2: "Brothers, if anyone is caught in any transgression, you who are spiritual should restore him in a spirit of

gentleness. Keep watch on yourself, lest you too be tempted. Bear one another's burdens and so fulfill the law of Christ."

How you handle these difficult situations is very important. With each conflict you handle you should grow and mature in your knowledge of working through conflict. James 1:2–5 gives us a good foundation for handling various trials:

> Count it all joy, my brothers, when you meet trials of various kinds, for you know that the testing of your faith produces steadfastness. And let steadfastness have its full effect, that you may be perfect and complete, lacking in nothing. If any of you lacks wisdom, let him ask God, who gives generously to all without reproach, and it will be given him.

In this passage James gives several principles concerning trials of various kinds. Our attitude should be one of joy in the midst of trouble, knowing that God is sovereign over all that is happening in our ministries. Note that this passage does not say *if* you have trials but *when* you have trials. In ministry you will have situations that will be difficult but it is good to know that God uses these trials to test our faith and grow us in holiness. Prayer is an important part of dealing with conflict or trials because God has promised to give us wisdom in the midst of the difficulty if we will ask for it. We should constantly be seeking his wisdom.

I believe the Lord allows conflict and other difficult situations in our worship ministry to conform us to the image of Christ (Rom 8:29). In the midst of conflict we need to be reminded of our own weaknesses and our need for the Spirit to intercede on our behalf. These times in ministry should keep us on our knees before the Lord, trusting him for the outcome. Rely on the Lord to give you wisdom and to walk with you through the difficult situations you find in ministry.

SECTION III

Preparing for Sunday

Chapter 15

Planning the Worship Service

ONE OF THE CENTRAL tasks for the worship minister is planning congregational worship. As we plan worship for our people each week we are actually engaged in pastoral care and discipleship. Our worship planning should go beyond simply "plugging in" songs to an already established template. Worship planning requires much prayer and thought if it is done well. Time alone with the Lord in prayer and study of the Scriptures should inform our worship planning.

As we plan we must be careful to remember the purpose of our gatherings. Why do we come together each week as the body of Christ? To begin, Scripture teaches us to do so. In Acts and the Epistles we have many examples of the church gathering together on a daily and weekly basis. We see in Hebrews 10:24–25 that brothers and sisters in Christ should "consider how to stir up one another to love and good works, not neglecting to meet together, as is the habit of some, but encouraging one another, and all the more as you see the Day drawing near." Regular meetings of the body of Christ are needed to build up believers.

We come together each week to exalt our God for who he is and what he has done for us in Christ. In our corporate worship services we rehearse the gospel story in Scripture, song, prayer, testimony, and preaching. We meet for fellowship and to celebrate the work of the Spirit in our lives. The weekly gathering of the church is a commemoration of all that the Lord is doing in the lives of the believers throughout the week.

Section III: Preparing for Sunday

There is great precedent in the New Testament for the church to meet often for worship. We also find many examples of what we should be doing in worship. In Acts we see that the believers met at regularly scheduled times. The ingredients of these meetings included teaching, evangelistic preaching, fellowship, breaking of break (Communion), prayers, times of praise, and commissioning of missionaries. Meetings were in the morning and evenings. The believers met on the first day of the week (Sunday) rather than the Sabbath.

In 1 Corinthians 14 we can also glean principles for worship planning. Much of the stress of this passage concerns the abuse of tongue speaking in the gatherings. The Corinth church was in a state of confusion when they gathered due to this issue. Paul instructs the leaders to plan and provide oversight so that the gathering is one of peace and not confusion (14:33). All things should be done properly and in an orderly manner (14:40). There is a strong emphasis on edification and exhortation in the gathering (14:3, 26). Old Testament worship at the tabernacle and temple tended to be more vertically focused between God and man. In the Epistles we see an added horizontal aspect that is centered on edifying the believers.

Paul reminds the church at Corinth to make sure all speech in the gatherings is intelligible (14:2–12) and that what is spoken in the meeting instructs the believers (14:19). In fact, Paul tells the Corinth congregation to hold those who are teaching accountable. Those in attendance must ensure that their leaders are teaching in accordance with Scripture (14:29). From this we can see the importance of study and preparation on the part of the preacher and the worship leader. Spontaneity may have its place occasionally in our gatherings but most of what we are doing should be well thought out in advance. Worship leaders need to be clear as they speak in the service, not allowing time to be spent on topics that are unrelated to the truths of Scripture.

Another important principle we learn from this passage concerns worship planning. Our worship gatherings should be participatory (14:26). All believers in this passage participate in the service. In this early church gathering the believers come prepared to share a psalm, a teaching, or a revelation. This is not a setting where the people sit passively watching their leaders do everything in the service. In our worship planning we should work diligently to involve the congregation in an active way in the service. Of course one of the best ways to actively involve the congregation in the worship service is through singing. We can also involve lay people through Scripture readings, prayers, and testimonies.

It is interesting that Paul acknowledges the presence of unbelievers in the gatherings of the Corinth church. Upon observing the believers singing and sharing about the Lord, an unbeliever is convicted and falls on his face worshiping God (14:25). This is a cue to worship planners to also consider the unbeliever in the service. The New Testament gatherings are primarily directed towards believers and as we plan our focus should be on edifying believers. Some churches determine to aim their services towards unbelievers as a church growth method. I would describe these services as evangelistic/seeker services, not worship services for believers.

Even though we plan our services for believers, what can we do to also speak to the unbeliever? I would not advocate "dumbing down" the service or avoiding certain topics because unbelievers are present. What we can do though is take time to explain what is happening in the service and define terms. When you have a prayer of confession, take a moment to explain why we should spend time confessing our sins. If the church is celebrating Communion or believer's baptism, spend a few moments describing the purpose of the ordinances. When we talk about sin, repentance, conversion, and sanctification, make mention of the meaning behind these terms. Even though we may intend to help an unbeliever in the service, it is possible that a believer could also be helped. In our worship planning keep in mind that ultimately it is the Holy Spirit who opens the eyes of the unbeliever to see the glorious gospel, not us. This does not excuse us from being mindful of unbelievers as we plan and lead worship.

In Old Testament worship at the tabernacle and temple the priest was the mediator between God and his people. This priest was an imperfect mediator because of his own sinful nature. When making a sacrifice for the people, the priest had to first offer a sacrifice for himself. Old Testament worship points ahead to a day when there would be a full and final sacrifice and a new mediator before the throne of God. Jesus' death as the Lamb of God ended the need for Old Testament sacrifices. His atoning death on the cross and resurrection changed how we worship forever. Jesus, our great high priest, makes it possible for us to "draw near to the throne of grace, that we may receive mercy and find grace to help in time of need" (Heb 4:14–16).

We must always keep before us that there is only one mediator in worship: Jesus Christ. How does this central truth impact our worship planning and leading? Since Jesus is our great high priest and the only mediator before God, we must be sure in our planning to keep the gospel present and clear in the service. There is no such thing as unmediated worship. We reflect on the work of Christ in our singing, praying, teaching, and preaching. It is possible for us to imply that there is another mediator in worship, such as music. When we expect our music to "usher us into the presence of God," we attempt to make music the mediator. Worship leaders must be on guard as they lead so as not to insinuate that they can lead the congregation into God's presence through their music or spoken words. The only person capable of bringing us into God's presence is his Son, Jesus, and for believers he has already done this (Eph 2:4–7; Heb 10:19–23; 12:22–24).

CONTENTS OF CORPORATE WORSHIP

As we consider worship planning think of the worship service in terms of *content*, *structure*, and *style*.[1] The content of the service focuses on what is said, sung, prayed, and preached. As we plan the content we seek to make the gospel the main attraction and the Scriptures prominent. The structure of the service concerns how the content or ingredients of the service are organized. The style of the service reflects the culture where the church is located. Style addresses the contextualization of the content. The style determines what kinds of songs are used and what instruments are played. Many times worship planners are more attentive to style when they should be more focused on the content and structure of the service.

There is not a passage in the New Testament that gives a structure or template for congregational worship, but we do have examples of what the early church did when they gathered. We can see the content of the worship gatherings as we look at Acts and the Epistles. Some of this content included congregational singing, Scripture reading, prayer, preaching/teaching, collections, Communion, baptism, electing leaders for the church, and commissioning of missionaries. Here are some thoughts on the specific content or elements of the worship service.

---

1. The earliest reference I know to this idea of content, structure, and style comes from the late Robert Webber, who taught and wrote about worship for many years. See his *Ancient-Future Faith*, 38.

SCRIPTURE

Worship services are based on the concept of revelation and response. God reveals himself to us and we respond to that revelation. A great example of this can be found in Isaiah 6, the call passage for the prophet Isaiah. Here Isaiah has a vision of the Lord in the temple. In his majesty and holiness the Lord reveals himself to Isaiah. Isaiah's response to this revelation is one of desperation as he realizes his own sinfulness before the Lord. Isaiah states that he is a man of unclean lips living among a people of unclean lips. In the next moment we see an angelic being flying to Isaiah with a burning coal from the altar of burnt sacrifice. He touches Isaiah's lips and tells him his guilt is taken away and his sin is atoned for. The Lord asks Isaiah to carry a message to the people. Isaiah responds, "Here I am, send me." In this commissioning service for the prophet Isaiah we see the pattern of revelation and response. God reveals himself and Isaiah responds.

As we plan worship, keep in mind that the only place where God's revelation occurs in the service is when Scripture is read, sung, and preached.[2] Everything else in the service functions as our response to God's revelation. If we fail to include Scripture in the service, we are shutting off God's revelation to his people. We expect our pastor to read and unpack the Scripture for us in his sermon, but as important as the sermon is in worship we clearly need to be incorporating more Scripture throughout the service.

The Apostle Paul instructs Timothy that "All Scripture is breathed out by God and profitable for teaching, for reproof, for correction, and for training in righteousness, that the man of God may be complete, equipped for every good work" (2 Tim 3:16–17). Scripture must have a special role in our services. The great Reformer Martin Luther (1483–1546) saw the importance of Scripture in the worship service when he said:

---

2. In 1 Corinthians 14 Paul argues the importance of the clear language of prophesying in the service rather than tongue speaking that is not interpreted. He warns though that this prophesying may be fallible and seeks for the believers to hold the person speaking accountable (14:29). Some may see this "prophesying" as a word or revelation from the Lord for that gathering. Others see it as teaching or preaching. It is clear, however, that anything shared in the service must align with Scripture. This makes Scripture the filter for anything that is spoken in the service by the pastor, other leaders, or lay persons. There is no new revelation outside of what Scripture teaches. One church I know that allows persons to share a prophesy (or word from the Lord) in the service first requires that person to speak to an elder or minister. The elder then determines if the person can share that word in the service based on its scriptural fidelity.

> This is the sum of the matter: that everything should be done so that the Word prevails . . . We can spare everything except the Word. We profit by nothing so much as by the Word. For the whole of Scripture shows that the Word should have free course among Christians. And in Luke 10, Christ himself says: "One thing is needful"—that Mary sit at the feet of Christ and daily hear his Word.[3]

As we plan and lead worship, we should read the Scripture, pray the Scripture, meditate upon the Scripture, and preach the Scripture.

SERMON

Sometimes people view the service in two parts: the worship and then the sermon. It is helpful if we view the total gathering as worship, including the sermon. We worship the Lord through the preaching of his Word. The sermon is a vital, essential part of the corporate worship time because it is the main place in the service for God's revelation to us. The pastor's sermon brings great focus to God's Word and its application to believers. As a general rule, when the church is gathered for corporate worship preaching should have a major role in that service. In your worship planning make sure there is adequate time allotted for the sermon to be presented in an unhurried manner. Work closely with your pastor as you shape the service so that he is satisfied with the order that precedes the message. If you have a pastor who plans his sermons weeks in advance, let this inform your worship planning.

PRAYERS

Sometimes I am surprised when I visit services that there are so few times of prayer. Prayer is our response to God and there should be several prayers interspersed throughout the service. Prayers in the service have different functions. There can be a prayer early in the service that is focused on adoration. Other prayers may be centered on confession of sins or intercession for needs of the congregation. There are offertory prayers, prayers for illumination (that we would understand God's Word), prayers of commitment, and prayers of benediction. As you plan the service, designate the purpose

---

3 Thompson, *Liturgies of the Western Church*, 98.

of each prayer. When you include lay people as prayer leaders, be sure they know the purpose of the prayer they are leading. When you are leading a prayer for the congregation, take some time to thoughtfully prepare the prayer. Consider writing out the prayer in advance. You do not have to read the prayer in the service but having thought through the wording of the prayer helps you when you pray. An effective way to pray in worship is to pray Scripture. Use one of the psalms, doxologies, or confessions found in the Bible as the foundation for your prayer.

SONGS

R. W. Dale, an English pastor from the nineteenth century, understood the importance of selecting songs for worship when he said, "Let me write the hymns and the music of the church, and I care very little who writes the theology. Heresy and Orthodoxy alike have in past ages discovered and used the power of sacred song."[4] Dale said this because Christians learn much of their theology through worship songs. This makes the selection of songs for worship a critical part of worship planning. When we select songs for worship the temptation is to select what is popular.

Obviously, the first consideration for selecting a worship song is not its popularity but its theological content. Every worship song or hymn is making theological statements. Are these statements grounded in Scripture? Is the meaning of the song crystal clear or vague? Is the lyric unbiblical? When determining the use of a worship song, we must be sure we are "rightly handling the word of truth"(2 Tim 2:15). We need to resist using a popular worship song (or even an old hymn) if it does not first pass the test of being theologically sound. Often we may find a song that passes the theological test except for one phrase. In my opinion that one phrase disqualifies the song. There are so many great worship songs we can use; why settle for a song with a questionable lyric?

Effective song lyrics are written in clear, intelligible language (1 Cor 14:19). The song should be worded in such a way that it speaks of the Lord the way the Bible speaks of the Lord. Song lyrics do not need to express scriptural concepts and themes with new images that could degrade the holiness of God.

Avoid lyrics that are vague in meaning. As a worship leader you only have a certain number of minutes in the service to sing gospel truths; why

---

4. Dale, *Nine Lectures on Preaching: Delivered at Yale*, 271.

spend time singing songs that are ambiguous? A dear worship leading friend used to say that he would not use any song in worship that could be sung in a cult setting due to the song's vagueness or lack of gospel truth. Do not waste your congregational worship time with worthless songs that have great chords and rhythm but no content.

The Apostle Paul in Colossians 3:16 reminds us to use a variety of songs (psalms, hymns, and spiritual songs). Not every song has to be a theological treatise. Some may be expressing a simple truth about the Lord. Just as a person strives to eat a balanced diet, we strive for balance in the types of worship songs we choose. Our songs can have both a vertical and a horizontal function since some exalt the Lord while others may be focused on encouraging the believers. The songs we choose should teach and admonish the congregation (Col 3:16). Worship leaders disciple their congregations by choosing songs that teach the great truths of the gospel.

As you plan your songs, choose songs that are easy for your congregation to sing. Songs that have simple rhythms and a comfortable range work well. If your congregation cannot seem to learn a new song after it has been sung several times, the problem is probably not with your congregation but with the song. Look to see if the text and musical setting go well together.

Ask yourself if the song is overly subjective or sentimental. Endeavor to find songs that accent the objective truths of the Word with a balanced subjective response. Most hymns do a great job of expressing objective truth. Ground your congregation in the objective truth of God's Word rather than seeking for an emotional subjective response. If your people are reminded of the greatness of God or the amazing news of the gospel through a song, they will respond subjectively with an outpouring of praise.

Discover worship songs that communicate the gospel well. It is difficult for one song to tell all the wonder of the gospel, but a gospel-centered song should unpack some aspect of the cross of Christ, his suffering, our sin, Christ's atonement, his grace, our redemption, and our hope because of the resurrection. We need more songs like these in our worship services.

As you select songs for worship, aim to balance familiar and unfamiliar songs. Consider using only one new song a service. Plan to introduce a new song each month to your congregation and at the end of the year they will know twelve new songs. Of course you will need to continue revisiting those songs in worship so they stay familiar to the congregation.

COMMUNION

Although the New Testament does not tell us how often we should practice Communion, some churches have weekly Communion while others observe it less often. Many of the newly established protestant churches during the Reformation moved away from weekly Communion due to the abuses that were associated with Communion. The Reformers wanted the church to take a biblical approach to the practice of Communion in corporate worship. Among Roman Catholic churches Communion became a works-oriented, salvific action and the main focus of the whole worship service.

Much care should be given to the observance of Communion or the Lord's Supper. In churches that observe weekly Communion, the practice can take on less of a priority simply because it is offered each week. Churches that offer it once a month or once a quarter should take care to not "tack on" the Communion to the end of the service when the congregation is anxious to leave. If Communion is placed at the end of the service, ensure there is appropriate time allotted for the observance.

Usually your pastor will lead the Communion time and you as the worship planner will decide how it is placed in the service. You also need to be thoughtful about how music will be used at the Communion. As your pastor begins the Communion time, he should "fence the table." At this point your pastor briefly explains the meaning of Communion and then clarifies who should take Communion. Communion is for believers only. In 1 Corinthians 11:17–34 Paul gives guidelines for observance of Communion.

Since my church observes Communion once a month, we often theme the whole service towards the Communion time. The early part of the service may feature a time of confession of sins along with an assurance of pardon. This is achieved through a prayer, Scripture reading, or a worship song or two. The songs and sermon centers on the cross of Christ. Since Communion has a sense of looking back at what Christ has done for us and looking forward to when he comes again, we end the service with a song that celebrates the finished work of Christ.

Section III: Preparing for Sunday

BAPTISM

Believer's baptism is a great time for the congregation to be encouraged about the work of the Lord in their midst. They see how he is changing lives and adding to the church. When your church schedules a baptism, give the baptism time a special place in the service. If your pastor is leading this part of the service, he will probably want the baptism scheduled early in the service. This will help him return to the service in time to prepare for the sermon. Many churches allow enough time in the service for baptismal candidates to share their conversion testimony. This can be accomplished through a previously recorded video or even by having a family member or friend read a written testimony. At one church the candidate gives a brief testimony from the baptism pool prior to the baptism. I would encourage you to consider scheduling a testimony time. As the congregation hears this new believer share, it is a powerful witness of the life-changing work of Christ. Your pastor will want to preview the baptismal candidate's written testimony several days before the service so he can make suggestions on length and wording of the testimony.

SUGGESTIONS ON WEEKLY WORSHIP PLANNING

As a worship leader you are planning worship every week and sometimes for more than one service if your church has a Wednesday or Sunday evening service. To help with the weekly planning, consider working several weeks ahead of time on your planning. One worship leader I know attempts to stay six weeks ahead on his worship planning. If your pastor gives you a list of upcoming sermons, you can use this information to shape the services. Plan ahead for Communion services, special occasions, and seasonal music for Christmas or Easter. By planning several weeks in advance, you can also schedule your worship team in advance. Have your worship and tech team members give you their availability for the month ahead. Set the worship team participants for the month.

Select songs and Scriptures for the upcoming six weeks and as you plan ahead remember to be flexible. Each week as you review your plan for the upcoming Sunday you may need to make some adjustments due to time constraints or a change in direction for that service. You may also decide to change to a different song that fits better in the service. Even though you plan in advance, you still work weekly to make sure the service is ready and

Planning the Worship Service

all details are covered. Planning ahead takes the pressure off of the weekly planning time. You already have an order of service planned and worship team members scheduled. You just need to make final adjustments.

Your weekly and advanced planning times should flow out of your personal devotion times with the Lord. As you sit down to plan worship, bathe the time in prayer and Scripture reading. Ask the Lord to help you as you plan. Make an effort to put away distractions as you pray through the services. If you are working in the church office, let the receptionist know that you do not want to be disturbed for the next couple of hours. Worship planning for your congregation deserves your best efforts and should not be hurried. I would always work to get services for the upcoming Sunday planned by Monday of that week. On Tuesday, I would revisit the plan to see if I had forgotten something or discovered a better way to order the elements. I would also make sure my pastor saw the service to get his thoughts on the worship plan. By Wednesday the service would be set and I would begin preparing for Wednesday night worship team rehearsals. Occasionally, there might be a change on Thursday or Friday but this was rare. If my pastor came to me at the end of the week with a request for the worship service, I would make this happen if at all possible.

After considering the content or ingredients of a worship service, some consideration should be given to the ordering of these elements. In the next two chapters there will be a discussion on the structure of the worship service—how it is ordered.

CHAPTER 16

Shaping the Order of Worship

THERE ARE MANY IMPORTANT elements that should be included in the corporate worship hour each week, such as singing, praying, reading Scripture and preaching. In the evangelical church the worship minister and the pastor play an important role in organizing these elements into a worship service. Through the ages there have been a number of worship orders used in the Christian church and there is something we can learn from each of the traditions. What are some of the typical structures churches use to order their worship?

LITURGICAL SERVICE

Justin Martyr (100–165) was a Roman philosopher who later converted to Christianity, defended the faith, and died a martyr. He gives us a glimpse into second-century worship gatherings. In one of his letters describing a Christian worship service Martyr mentions that the first part of the service centered on reading "memoirs of the apostles or the writings of the prophets," followed by preaching. The second part of the service was an observance of Communion.[1] We notice in early Christian worship the development of a two-part service: service of the Word and service of the table. Studying orders of worship for the next few centuries reveals a similar two-part structure except that the services became more elaborate as they included many different prayers and songs. This particular two-part

---

1. Thompson, *Liturgies of the Western Church*, 3–10.

structure is commonly referred to as a liturgical service.[2] The order would include Scripture readings from the Old Testament, an Epistle, and a Gospel. All liturgical services include Communion. Often in the churches that use this structure (service of the Word, service of the table) the preaching is minimalized while Communion becomes the main focus. In liturgical-type churches (Roman Catholic, Episcopal, Anglican, Greek Orthodox) the order of worship is influenced by the liturgical church calendar and the lectionary. The calendar determines what types of songs and prayers would be used according to the liturgical season (such as Advent, Christmas, Epiphany, Lent, Easter, Pentecost). The lectionary is a three- to five-year plan of Scripture readings to be used each week in worship.

One of the worthy traits of a liturgical service is the amount of Scripture reading incorporated in the service. The negative aspects of this type service are a lack of interpreting these Scriptures for the people and a low view of preaching. Many liturgical churches also have a theological view of Communion (transubstantiation) that would be recognized as unscriptural in evangelical church settings.[3] It is possible to use a liturgical-type order and improve on the deficits. The structure of this service is acceptable when preaching has its proper place in the service and the Communion is viewed biblically.

A SIMPLE LITURGICAL SERVICE ORDER

- Prelude
- Processional hymn/song
- Greeting and opening prayer
- *Kyrie eleison* ("Lord have mercy")—usually sung
- Assurance of pardon
- *Gloria in excelsis Deo* ("Glory to God in the highest")—usually sung

---

2. The root word for liturgy is the Greek word *leitourgia*, meaning service. Paul uses this Greek word in Romans 12:1 when describing worship. Worship is seen as service to the Lord.

3. Transubstantiation is the view of Communion that sees the bread and wine as the actual body and blood of Christ. Before observing the Communion the presiding priest prays for the Holy Spirit to transform the elements into the physical body and blood of Christ. This unbiblical view was a major issue among the Reformers in the sixteenth century.

SECTION III: PREPARING FOR SUNDAY

- Old Testament reading
- Responsorial psalm
- New Testament reading (Epistle)
- Alleluia and gospel procession
- Gospel reading
- Sermon
- Credo (creed)—spoken together
- Prayers of the people (bidding prayers)
- Offertory (giving of gifts)
- Prayer of thanksgiving ("The Lord be with you")
- *Sanctus* and *Benedictus* ("Holy, Holy, Holy"/"Blessed is he who comes in the name of the Lord")
- The Lord's Prayer
- Passing of the peace
- *Agnus Dei* ("Lamb of God who takes away the sins of the world")
- Communion procession (coming forward to partake of the elements)
- Blessing/benediction
- Recessional hymn/song
- Postlude

THEMATIC SERVICE

A thematic service brings focus on one particular theme that flows throughout the whole service. Some worship planners use this type of worship planning when the pastor desires for the songs and Scripture readings to be themed with his message. For example, the pastor may be preaching on the Beatitudes from Matthew 5 so the songs and other Scripture readings will be aimed at that topic. This type of service works well during special seasons such as Christmas or Easter. If your pastor does not give you his sermon topics several weeks in advance, it may be difficult to use this structure. Thematic services can be especially challenging when there are really no songs that would match up with a particular topic. The thematic service should be used sparingly simply because there are other themes that need to be featured in a regular service besides the one theme. I will employ this thematic idea in a limited way by selecting the song before the sermon to go with the pastor's sermon.

GOSPEL-CENTERED SERVICE

The gospel-centered service uses a historic church worship order with a Christ-centered approach. In this type structure the service "should show the face of Jesus to those who have gathered and to those who need to gather to worship him."[4] This type of service, also called Christ-centered worship or cross-centered worship, arranges the service in the order of the gospel. Brian Chapell argues that our corporate worship time "is nothing more, and nothing less, than a representation of the gospel in the presence of God and his people for his glory and their good."[5] A typical order of worship would be:

- Adoration
- Confession
- Assurance
- Thanksgiving
- Petition and intercession
- Instruction
- (Communion)
- Response
- Benediction

At the beginning of the service the worship minister leads the congregation to consider the great God that we worship. Here there could be some combination that includes the reading of a psalm or other Scripture passage, a prayer of adoration, or a song of praise. Once we focus on the greatness and holiness of God we move to a confession time. At this point we realize that in the presence of a holy God we are sinful people in need of redemption. At the confession time the worship leader reads Scripture that describes our sinfulness and our need to repent, then leads the

---

4. Chapell, *Christ-Centered Worship*, 123.
5. Ibid., 120.

congregation in a confession prayer. There could also be a song of confession. The time for confession of sins in the service is followed by an assurance of pardon. The worship leader quotes a Scripture passage that reminds us of our redemption and hope in Christ, such as 1 John 1:9–10. Next, the time of Thanksgiving celebrates the work of Christ and our gratefulness for the salvation we have in him. This is followed by an intercessory prayer time often led by the pastor, then preaching, Communion, response, and a benediction.

Another possible approach to worship planning using the gospel-centered model is to structure your service under these headings: Creation, Fall, Redemption, Restoration or Praise, Renewal, Commitment. With these gospel-type structures there is freedom as to how you incorporate the different elements. Under each heading you could include Scripture, songs, or prayers. One week you may want to have a confession time where a song is the guide for the confession. Another week you could use Scripture and no song for the confession time. Even though you are following a framework, how you build around the framework can vary from week to week.

Many churches follow this gospel-centered structure, although not all churches feature Communion each week. This kind of service keeps the focus on Christ and not us. In our self-centered culture the accent is on our wants and needs. Sadly, many of our worship services today seem more man-centered than God-centered. Gospel-centered worship is a reminder each time the church gathers for worship of all that we have in Christ as we retell the gospel story in Scripture and song.

SONG-CENTERED WORSHIP SERVICE

Some churches follow a model of service that features a long music segment followed by preaching. In this structure a major portion of the service is given over to a number of worship songs sung in secession, with little or no spoken transitions or Scripture readings. Churches that use this structure may have a two-hour service where singing is the first hour followed by preaching in the second hour. Songs are sometimes ordered more by the tempo and style of the song than theme—faster songs flow to songs in a medium speed followed by slow, intimate worship songs. This model is found in a number of churches that tend to be more charismatic in nature. A positive trait of this type service is the opportunity for the congregation to spend a protracted period of time singing songs of praise. Many feel this type of service can be emotionally manipulative because of the methods employed in planning the worship. Songs are selected and ordered so that they will lead the congregation to a particular emotional response. Some of our more conservative evangelical churches use this model not knowing of its Pentecostal, charismatic roots. Here is a typical order of worship:

Song-Centered Worship
(Sometimes Referred to as Free-Flowing Praise)[6]

Based on Psalm 95

Song Service

Invitation—call to worship (verse 1)

Engagement—the people draw near to God (verse 2)

Exaltation—people sing out to the Lord (verses 3–5)

Adoration—songs are less upbeat (verse 6)

Intimacy—personal, quiet (verse 7)

Closeout

Preaching

Scripture reading

Sermon

Dismissal

There are a number of churches that follow some variety of this order of service. With all of the attention given to singing in this type of a service, other elements can be diminished, such as Scripture readings and prayers.

---

6. Liesch, *New Worship*, 54–58.

Section III: Preparing for Sunday

SCRIPTURE-GUIDED WORSHIP

Another structure worship planners employ is one that allows the Scripture to direct the ordering of the service. Scripture-guided worship takes a particular passage, such as a psalm or another selected Scripture passage, and allows the passage to organize the content of the service. Here is an explanation of this type worship structure.

> The helpful and unique quality inherent in Scripture-guided worship design is that a particular biblical passage provides not only the *structure* for the entire worship service, but also the *content*. The Scripture passage chosen (in most instances in connection to the sermonic text), informs everything included in the corporate gathering: songs choices, the focus of corporate prayer, transition statements between worship elements, other passages of Scripture utilized during the gathering, and even the dreaded announcements! While historical liturgies and lectionary structures (prescribed) are traditionally rich with Scripture readings and creeds, the Scripture-guided design is more flexible in addressing the specific rhythms and nuances of life unique to each church. Another significant aspect of Scripture-guided worship is the hermeneutical consistency associated with the analogy of faith. The analogy of faith is a principle of biblical interpretation built on the premise that Scripture interprets Scripture. Not only should Scripture be the fundamental authority for the sermon, and the guiding principle for the content and order of worship, but the Bible's own internal rhythm sets the paradigm for Scripture-guided worship.[7]

Below you will see two examples of a Scripture-guided worship.

Sunday Worship (Based on Psalm 46)

"God is our refuge and strength, a very present help in trouble." (46:1)

Hymn—"A Mighty Fortress Is Our God"

(During verses 3 and 4, instrumental only
—congregation will read 46:1–7)

---

7. Scripture-guided worship definition is from a correspondence with Dr. Joseph Crider, Professor of Church Music and Worship at The Southern Baptist Theological Seminary, Louisville, KY. He is the first to teach on this structure of worship and supplied the Scripture-guided worship examples for this chapter.

Shaping the Order of Worship

Song—"This Is Our God"

"Be still and know that I am God." (46:10)

Welcome and opening prayer
—a prayer of confession based on our sin of worry

Song—"He Will Hold Me Fast"

Song—"All I Have Is Christ"

"I will be exalted among the nations, I will be exalted in the earth!" (46:10)

Pastoral prayer and offering

Song—"How Marvelous"

"The Lord of hosts is with us; the God of Jacob is our fortress." (46:11)

Sermon

Worship in response

Song—"Cornerstone"

Church life and benediction

Sunday Worship (Based on Philippians 3)

"Rejoice in the Lord. To write the same things to you is no trouble to me and is safe for you." (3:1)

Song—"Come People of the Risen King"

Hymn—"Rejoice the Lord Is King"

"For we are the real circumcision, who worship by the Spirit of God and glory in Christ Jesus and put no confidence in the flesh." (3:3)

Welcome and prayer

Song—"There Is a Redeemer"

Song—"Your Name"

"But whatever gain I had, I counted as loss for the sake of Christ." (3:7)

Scripture reading and offertory prayer—3:7–16

Song—"Song of Grace"

". . . I press on to make it my own, because Christ Jesus has made me His own." (3:12)

Section III: Preparing for Sunday

Sermon—3:12–16

Worship in response

Song—"O Church Arise"

Church life and benediction

This particular structure of worship gives a priority to God's Word in the planning stages and within the service. We need more services that give an important place to Scripture.

RANDOM ORDER OF SERVICE

This is a service of unrelated elements that fit into the period of time allotted for worship. In this random-ordered service the worship leader is given an allotted time to plan the worship music and the pastor uses the remaining time for the message. There is no effort made to bring unity to the service through theme or service order. This model is the least desirable of the structures discussed in this chapter. A worship minister sometimes finds himself caught in this structure because there is little or no coordination between the worship minister and others who have input into the service.

Even serious worship planners can find themselves in this spot occasionally. On Monday the service is completed. It has a good flow, perhaps in a gospel-centered or Scripture-guided structure, but elements continue to be inserted into the plan. On Tuesday the pastor decides he wants to insert a video on stewardship so you choose the best spot in the service to do this. On Wednesday the children's minister asks to spend a few moments in the service announcing the new Vacation Bible School theme and date. On Thursday you find out that there will be a baptism added to the service and on Friday you discover that there will be a testimony about an upcoming mission trip. Each day you rework the order of service to accommodate these requests. As you make room for these new elements, other elements are eliminated due to time. By Friday the service you planned looks nothing like it did on Monday. The service now appears to be a service of random elements sandwiched together with no apparent flow and you feel like a game show host announcing what is coming next.

When you find yourself in this situation, the key is to be flexible. If it seems the situation is out of control, seek out your pastor, explain the situation, and get his thoughts. He may think it is too much to add all of those elements to the service and advise you to talk with those who asked for time. It could be that some of these new elements could be scheduled on other Sundays. It is helpful if you and your pastor agree on what items should be in the service and which ones should be shared in another way (slide announcement, bulletin, weekly newsletter). In the midst of all of this remember that the Lord can use these services just as well as the ones you have spent hours preparing. Sometimes the service you think will have the least impact is the one used by the Spirit to change lives. This is a good reminder to us that ultimately we can change no one's life through the order of service or our worship leading. God is the change agent.

CONCLUSION

There is no New Testament–sanctioned order of worship. We have a good list of elements of worship but not an order. This means we are free to order the service in a way that honors biblical principles of worship, giving priority to congregational singing, focus on the gospel, and reading and expositing the Scripture. Perhaps one of the worship structures discussed in this chapter fits well in your church. Some may want to adapt or blend structures. What works for one church may not work as well in another church. It is helpful, however, to study these worship structures and lean on these for guidance. Here we see a great heritage of worship practice. Planning the corporate worship time for your congregation is a serious responsibility. You are guiding your people in worship of the almighty God, creator of the heavens and the earth. You are helping your people understand who they are in Christ. You are preparing them for eternity.

CHAPTER 17

Planning Worship for Special Occasions

EVANGELICAL CHURCHES FOR THE most part do not follow the liturgical church calendar when planning worship, but there are still several Sundays each year that call for a different emphasis in worship. As we plan these services we want to keep in mind that the overall purpose of the worship service does not change and the focus remains on the greatness of our God and the wonder of the gospel.

CHRISTMAS

The Christmas season is a busy time in worship ministry. In addition to the normal Sunday worship services, there may be several special services to plan. Many churches schedule a Christmas musical featuring the worship choir and instrumentalists, a children's Christmas musical, and Christmas Eve services. The rehearsal preparation and coordination of these services can be overwhelming. These services should be put on the calendar early in the year. Advanced planning helps to relieve some of the stress of the Christmas season when it arrives.

Many churches will use a worship choir to prepare a special evening of Christmas music in December. There are several options when considering an evening like this. One option is using a newly published Christmas musical. These musicals range in difficulty and length. They also have orchestra or worship band charts available as well as prerecorded tracks. Today many of these musicals come with click tracks that make it possible for the worship band to accompany along with prerecorded orchestral instruments. Another option when considering a special Christmas music service is for you to create a service using a combination of worship choir songs, congregational songs, and songs that feature the worship band with Scripture. You could also plan a traditional evening of Christmas music using a lessons-and-carols format.

Whatever the plan for this evening, it is best to choose the music in the summer and begin rehearsing the music with your groups in August or early September. Consider having a weekend retreat on a Friday night and Saturday morning when you introduce the Christmas music and begin learning the music. I know a church that plans a "Christmas in August" retreat each year. They decorate the rehearsal area with Christmas decorations including a Christmas tree and serve Christmas-themed refreshments.

SELECTING CHRISTMAS SONGS FOR WORSHIP

Each year we have the opportunity to use the traditional carols and some newer Christmas worship songs. When it comes to Christmas carols and worship songs, they are not all created equal. Here are several principles to consider when choosing songs for Christmas worship services.

1. Check the biblical accuracy of the Christmas song. Does the song text agree with Scripture? We take this for granted since we sing many of these Christmas songs every year. All of your songs should first pass through a theological filter.

2. Avoid songs with vague lyrics. Is the message of the song clear? If you cannot decipher a song lyric's meaning, your congregation will most likely not understand it either.

3. Resist the desire to choose songs because of sentimental attachment, especially if the words are weak. Perhaps this Christmas song with weak lyrics needs to be retired from congregational worship at your church.

4. Balance Christmas hymns and songs that have strong theological content with those that are more simple songs of praise.

5. Look for Christmas songs that explain why Christ came to earth. Find songs that are not only focused on the birth of Christ but tell the whole story. You will have many guests at Christmas services that need to know that Jesus died for their sins, rose again, and now reigns

victoriously over sin and death. People need to see their need for a Savior not just the babe in the manger.

6. Avoid the secular songs of the season. There is so much about the Christmas season that leans toward commercialism and Santa Claus. Keep the focus on Christ.

The pastor of the first church I served as a worship minister used to anxiously wait for the Christmas season to pass because he said people were not focused on the gospel but on the many other distractions of the Christmas season. We must strive to keep Christ in Christmas especially as we plan our services.

EASTER (HOLY WEEK)

Easter and the week leading up to Easter often will include special worship services. Perhaps your church has a special emphasis on Palm Sunday, Maundy Thursday, or Good Friday. Palm Sunday commemorates the triumphal entry of Christ in Jerusalem. In the churches where I served we would not focus a whole service on the Palm Sunday theme but would acknowledge the significance of the day through Scripture reading or a worship song.

A Maundy Thursday service is a traditional service held on the Thursday before Easter. Its name is derived from the Latin phrase *mandatum novum*, which means "a new commandment." In the Gospel of John Jesus washes his disciples' feet and shares the Passover meal. On this evening he also tells them, "A new commandment I give to you, that you love one another: just as I have loved you, you also are to love one another" (John 13:34). Ancient Maundy Thursday services included foot washing and the Lord's Supper, but most of these services today focus on the Lord's Supper.

Good Friday services are sometimes held from noon to 3:00 p.m. and would include a service of music and Scripture readings focused on the sufferings of Christ on the cross. Some services are planned around the seven last words of Christ taken from the Gospels. Churches may also have a Good Friday service in the evening.

Many churches plan an Easter sunrise service. Sometimes these services are held outside away from the church building. They require some coordination so that there is electric power, a sound system, and instruments available. Usually the musical portion of this kind of service is intentionally simple, with only an instrument or two and a worship leader.

As you plan for special services research traditional orders of service. Incorporate songs that are familiar to your congregation. For Easter Sunday consider adding some additional time to the service for singing and perhaps some additional instrumentalists. If your church normally uses a worship band on Sunday mornings, consider adding some orchestral instruments such as strings or brass to the Easter Sunday services as you celebrate Christ's resurrection.

PATRIOTIC SERVICES

Each Memorial Day, Independence Day, and Veterans Day some churches take time in their services to acknowledge the founding of the United States and to recognize those who have served or are serving in the military. I remember on one of these Sundays there was an honor guard processing with the American flag in the worship service. The congregation would say the pledge of allegiance, sing the national anthem and other patriotic songs, and then recognize veterans.

I love my country and am grateful to be an America citizen. I am also grateful to the many who have served and fought for the freedoms we enjoy everyday. Having said that, I do not believe many of the practices carried out in worship services around patriotic holidays have a place in worship. We can acknowledge our gratefulness to those who have served and fought so that we have the freedom to worship. We also should pray for our country and its leaders as Scripture tells us to do (1 Tim 2:1–4; Rom 13). In all of this the focus must remain on the Lord and not the country. In many of our churches today we have visitors who are from other countries. We do not want them to think that God is only partial to Americans. As much as we may love our country, our chief allegiance as Christians is not to the United States of America but to Jesus Christ. Let us pray for our leaders and show gratefulness to those who serve in our military for us, but as we plan these services let us keep the emphasis on Christ.

OTHER SPECIAL SERVICES

Many churches observe Mother's Day, Father's Day, parent-child dedications, and Graduate Sunday. It is easy for the focus of our worship services to be in the wrong place when we approach these days. Careful planning to acknowledge these days yet keep the focus on the Lord is essential. Certainly in our present culture we in the church need to do all we can do to encourage the Christian family. On these particular Sundays the most appropriate thing we can do is to pray for the family and to preach on the biblical view of the family.

CHAPTER 18

Leading and Evaluating the Worship Service

YOUR EFFECTIVENESS AS A worship leader on Sunday morning begins with the amount of preparation you do each week. Time spent meditating on the Word, praying, planning the service, leading rehearsals, and checking the technical equipment all impact Sunday. What are some practical suggestions on leading the worship service on Sunday?

DO YOUR HOMEWORK

Sometime during the week you need to get alone with the worship order and decide on transitions—anything you will say in service. Print these transitions and prepare your charts. Many worship leaders use an electronic notebook or something similar as they lead worship that includes their transitions and charts. I use a three-ring binder and put everything in order in the binder for Sunday with personal notes that remind me of the order and other things such as using or removing a capo. Practice your songs and transitions. Read the Scripture readings out loud to be sure you can pronounce all of the words well.

WORSHIP BEFORE YOU LEAD WORSHIP

Spend time worshiping the Lord privately as you work on your songs and transitions. On Sunday morning your chief responsibility is to lead your congregation. You will have many things on your mind as you guide the congregation through the service. Sometimes you will not feel like you have worshiped due to the distractions you have as the worship leader. Worship the Lord as you rehearse the service in preparation for Sunday and serve your congregation as you lead the service.

ARRIVE RESTED

One church I served a number of years ago had three Sunday morning services each week. This required me as the worship leader to arrive at the church very early on Sunday morning to prepare for the day. I quickly realized the importance of getting a good night's rest on Saturday. Sometimes due to illness or young children waking up in the middle of the night you may not sleep well and begin your Sunday in an energy deficit. These days are unavoidable and serve to remind us that we are weak and in need of the Spirit's power every Sunday. On Saturday evenings be intentional about getting to bed early.

SET THE EXAMPLE

If you ask your worship and tech team to arrive at a particular time on Sunday mornings, you need to be there before they arrive. Make sure you have completed any preparation you need to accomplish before they arrive. Do not make them wait on you to be ready. If you do not start on time, your team will start coming later to rehearsal.

CHECK PROJECTION MEDIA

Be sure to check all song slides and other projected media in advance of Sunday morning. You may notice at rehearsal on Sunday morning that one word is wrong or misspelled. Designate some of your vocalists to check the slides as you rehearse the songs prior to the service. Do not let your songslides be a distraction in worship.

BATHE THE MORNING IN PRAYER

Spend time in prayer and confession prior to coming to the church on Sunday morning. Arrive spiritually ready to lead your team and congregation. Pray with your tech team and worship team before beginning the rehearsal. Pray again before the service starts. If possible, pray with your pastor prior to the service. No matter how cleverly or creatively you craft the order of service or rehearse the team, nothing happens in the service unless the Holy Spirit does a work in your midst.

KNOW YOUR SONGS

Ideally, it would be great to lead the service with no song charts in front of you. Some worship leaders do this. I personally do not trust myself, but I do know that I need to be overly familiar with the charts before the service. If you are accompanying yourself on guitar or piano, know your chord progressions well. All of this preparation will help you improve your eye contact with the congregation.

BE EXPRESSIVE

You may think that effective communication with the congregation as you lead the service is contingent on how you sing, speak, or play your instrument. This is true but a great part of your communication is also dependent on how you express yourself physically. This includes your posture, eye contact, facial expression, and clothing. Leading with good posture is important when singing because it supports production of a healthy vocal tone. Your posture also communicates what you think about your message. Singing and speaking from a good posture shows confidence in the truth you are sharing. If you lead from guitar, adjust your boom stand so that you are not leaning over to reach the microphone. If you lead from a piano bench make sure your boom stand is adjusted so you are sitting straight.

I sometimes see worship leaders who close their eyes most of the time they are leading worship. I understand the desire to communicate your heart to the Lord by concentrating on him and closing your eyes, but have you considered how much you communicate to the congregation through your eyes? This is a major place of expression for you as a worship leader. Also, by keeping your eyes open you are more aware of your environment.

You can be sensitive to what may be happening on the platform or in the congregation or with the technical equipment. The most important places to have good eye contact with your congregation are at the beginning of verses and other critical points in the song (beginning of a chorus, bridge, or tag). The congregation is depending on you to lead them into the song at the right time. Your eye contact can make sure this happens. Most worship leaders are tempted to look down at their charts at the crucial times they should be looking out at the congregation. Keep looking ahead at your chart then look out at your people.

Many worship leaders think they have good facial expression when they really do not. Your face needs to reflect the song texts to your congregation. If you tend to be shy in public, you must come out of your shell when you lead worship. Ask a trusted friend or staff member at church to tell you how you are doing with facial expression. Also, consider video recording your service and evaluate your own worship leadership. I often tell my team that if they think they are being expressive, they probably are not. They need to go to that next level of expressiveness where they are perhaps a little uncomfortable. In all of this discussion on expression we want to be sure that our expression is authentic. Your expression should always be heartfelt.

Be considerate of how you dress to lead worship. At most churches the worship team leads from a platform that is several feet higher than the congregation. Everything your wear is magnified by the height of the platform and the focused lighting. Your shoes may actually be at eye level for your congregation. One of our goals as worship leaders is to not be a distraction in worship. Clothing that may be seen as sensual in nature has no place on the platform (or at church). Your church should have a dress code for the worship team that outlines for men and women what is appropriate apparel on the platform. The best time to communicate appropriate dress issues is before there is a problem. New team members need to know the dress code prior to their first week serving.

SPEAK EFFECTIVELY

Worship leaders should plan every word they are going to say in the worship service in advance. If you desire to be more spontaneous and not plan transitions ahead of time, you are setting yourself up for an embarrassing moment when you say something that you did not mean to say. Or you may say something that can have more than one meaning. I am not advocating for you to read word for word what you have in your notes. The main point is that you have given thoughtful planning to what you will say. Let your notes guide your speaking.[1]

As you plan your transitions do not assume that people understand why you have arranged the order of worship a certain way or why you selected a particular song. Explain the meaning of the confession prayer or offering time. Tell them why they need to sing the particular song you have selected.

As you speak in the service, remember that people cannot listen as fast as you can speak. Slow down and be expressive in your speech. Integrate Scripture into your transitions as much as possible. Make your transitions concise. You are not the preacher. Sometimes you do not need to say anything, but simply lead the congregation in the song.

EVALUATE THE WORSHIP SERVICE

After each Sunday take time to evaluate the worship services. This is an important step to growth in your worship leading and your worship team's development. Here are some questions to consider:

- How did the service flow?
- Was I organized and prepared to lead?
- Did my transitions, prayers, or Scripture readings go well?
- Were song entrances effective?
- Was the music well executed?
- Was the worship team on time and ready?
- Did all of the technical equipment work?
- Were the song slides correct and easy to read?
- What needs to be fixed before the next service?
- What comments did I receive from my pastor, staff, or lay people that need action?

1. There can be a place for spontaneity in your worship leading. You and your pastor need to have a prior understanding about possible times that may call for adjusting what is planned in the service. It could be that your pastor wants to be the one who decides this in a service and leads this time.

Section III: Preparing for Sunday

One of my major prayers when preparing to lead worship is that I would not be a distraction. We want our people focused on the Lord and not us. When things don't go well in the service, the focus is often more on us than the Lord. Something that was a problem in a service one week should be corrected before the next week.

Effectiveness as a worship leader greatly depends on your diligence in planning and preparing to lead the services week in and week out. Each week in the service there is always something we had hoped would go better. There is no perfect service because we are not perfect people, but we constantly strive for excellence in our preparation and in our leading. Careful evaluation helps you improve your leadership.

CHAPTER 19

Worship Leading for Life

NONE OF US KNOWS how long we will serve in worship ministry. Many worship leaders begin serving in worship ministry while in college and continue to retirement. The Lord may lead others down different paths of ministry after a few years. Whether on the front end of ministry or towards the end, worship leaders should take care of their health so they can serve faithfully for many years. If you do not steward the physical abilities you have, at some point you may not be able to function in your role as a worship minister.

We discussed earlier about the importance of the daily spiritual disciplines in the life of the worship minister. These are non-negotiable. We must make time to be immersed in the Scriptures and devoted to prayer. An often-neglected area beyond the spiritual disciplines is our physical health. How we take care of our bodies also impacts our effectiveness for ministry. We may have some physical ailments that come to us that we cannot control, but our diet, exercise, and rest patterns are fundamentals we can control. If we are not careful, the busyness of our ministries and family responsibilities can cause us to compromise our own health.

It makes sense that if you are eating poorly, not getting enough rest, and lacking regular exercise, you may also not be functioning well in your work. At these points you may even be making poor ministry and family decisions due to your health. If we are not taking care of ourselves, we cannot give to our families and church members as we would like. Recently I was talking with a young worship leader who mentioned that he felt out of control in all of these areas and because of this he also felt he was not effectively leading his family and church. He decided that he had to improve his diet, exercise, and rest. This required a reexamining of his daily and weekly schedule.

It is helpful if your church will allow you to have a day off during the week since Sunday is not really a day of rest for the minister. Friday was usually my day off when serving in full-time ministry. There were Fridays when a church event was planned but for the most part I was able to be away from the office on Friday. A day off during the week is good for your mental health as you get away from the office, email, voicemail, messaging, and social media. You can work around your house, spend time with your family, or develop a hobby that helps you to relax.

When my children were young, I sometimes watched them at home on Fridays so my wife could get out of the house to run errands or do some things she wanted to do without the children. I also found working in the yard an enjoyable activity on my day off. As a child I despised yard work, but as an adult I found yard work relaxing. I enjoyed seeing the results of a day of cutting grass and trimming shrubbery, which is so different from ministry. The work of the ministry often feels incomplete and it is sometimes difficult to see results. If you have the opportunity to take a day off during your week of ministry, let it be your Sabbath rest.

Sometimes when I am stressed in my work I discover that the stress is multiplied by my "out of control" lifestyle. I am not handling things well. Eating well, exercising several times a week, and getting to bed earlier help me to deal with stressful situations more effectively. All of this is a matter of discipline and getting control of the schedule. We all know these principles to be true and yet do little to make the changes we need to make. What will you do to get these areas of life under control?

VOCAL HEALTH

Professional singers can develop serious vocal issues. The bad vocal habits some professional singers develop in their early years of work can cause them to lose their vocal abilities within ten years. Worship ministers rely heavily on their ability to speak and sing. Can you imagine trying to do your work without a well-functioning voice? Each week we speak and sing in multiple rehearsals and sometimes multiple services. What are the basic disciplines we should seek to keep our voices in good shape for years to come? You must be a good steward of the vocal ability the Lord has given you to use in his service. Here are a few important vocal principles to put into practice.

1. Your voice works best when you are rested. Getting enough sleep on Saturday night is so important to how you will function vocally on Sunday.

2. Before you begin singing on Sunday morning or at a rehearsal, take time to warm up your voice. This is similar to stretching before you start exercising. Humming in a comfortable range is a great way to start. Vocal slides up and down by fifths or octaves on an "Ah" [a] vowel in a comfortable range are another good way to begin. Once you do these slides continue expanding into your lower and upper range but stay relaxed. Begin singing one of your easier songs scheduled for the service or rehearsal. All the while you warm up, monitor if you are relaxed and if there is a feeling of ease in your voice rather than tension.

3. Check to see how you are breathing. Focus on producing a low breath. Your chest should not be moving up and down as you sing. Set your posture and breathe low.

4. How is your posture? If you lead from guitar or piano, adjust your boom stand so that you are not leaning over to sing. Your goal is a tall straight stance as you sing. Pretend you have a puppet string pulling at the top of your head that is aligning your head, neck, and chest. Your vocal track works best when your posture is well aligned.

5. Can you hear yourself sing when the instruments are playing? You could be causing vocal strain by over-singing if you do not hear yourself well. Work to have your monitor adjusted so that you can hear yourself sing well above the instruments.

6. Are you drinking plenty of water? You may have a habit of drinking coffee or a soft drink while rehearsing or leading worship. This does not substitute for water. In fact, did you know that caffeinated drinks actually dehydrate you? Always have a water bottle nearby and be sure to stay hydrated throughout a rehearsal or worship service.

7. Are you singing in a vocal range that works well with your voice? If you are a bass singer trying to sing high tenor notes, you are putting extra strain on your voice. Be sure to pitch your worship songs in a

comfortable range for your congregation. This will also help you as you lead the song.

SOME VOCAL WARNING SIGNS

1. Does your voice hurt when you sing high notes for a period of time? You are probably experiencing excess tension and need help learning to access those upper notes in a relaxed way. This could also be a result of not warming up your voice before the rehearsal or service. If it hurts to sing, something is not right.

2. Is there a part of your range where your voice does not work? I'm not referring to the notes that are simply out of your range but notes that you should be able to sing. Are there several notes in the middle of your range that do not work well? You probably need to be seen by a doctor who can check to see if you have damage to your vocal folds.

3. Do you constantly experience sinus drainage that causes you to clear your voice every few minutes? Clearing your voice can be detrimental over a long period of time. Perhaps you need to be checked for allergies to see if you can alleviate the sinus drainage.

4. If you are experiencing a sore throat due to illness, you need to be careful that you do not damage your vocal folds as you sing. If you have a sore throat and a fever you should not sing. Basically, if it hurts to phonate (talk or sing) do not sing.

5. Are you hoarse after a rehearsal or a worship service? This can be due to excess tension while you sing. It is common for your voice to be tired but not for your voice to be hoarse after a service. If this continues over a period of time, you should find a voice teacher or speech pathologist to help you discover what is causing the hoarseness.

When you are experiencing any of these symptoms, you may need to seek professional help. Discover an ENT doctor in your area that works with singers. This person can look at your vocal folds with a scope and give you advice as to the health of your singing voice.

HEARING HEALTH

Can you imagine trying to do your worship ministry work without good hearing? I once had a sound technician who had hearing damage. He actually could not hear some upper frequencies. This was a definite problem when the sound system feedback was in a range he could not hear. You may not lose your ability to hear, but if you are not protecting your hearing you could lose the ability to hear certain frequencies. Vocal health is important and so is hearing health for the worship minister.

SOME PRINCIPLES TO CONSIDER ON HEARING HEALTH:

1. If you are listening to loud music, you could be damaging your hearing. If your hearing is dull after a concert, you are experiencing damage to your hearing. Your ears may recover by the next day, but the damage may not show up for years.
2. According to a document put out by the National Association of Schools of Music, sounds over 85 decibels (dB), such as the sound of a vacuum cleaner, can put you at the greatest risk of hearing damage.[1]
3. Hearing damage is determined by the *sound level* and the *length of time* you are exposed to the sound (volume and duration). Here is a list of maximum daily exposure times for sounds when protecting your hearing. The times listed below indicate how long you can be exposed to this level of sound before you experience hearing damage.

    - 85 dB (vacuum cleaner, MP3 player at 1/3 volume)—8 hours
    - 90 dB (hair dryer, blender)—2 hours
    - 94 dB (MP3 player at 1/2 volume)—1 hour
    - 100 dB (MP3 player at full volume, lawnmower)—15 minutes
    - 110 dB (rock concert, power tools)—2 minutes
    - 120 dB (jet plane at takeoff)—without ear protection sound damage is almost immediate[2]

---

1. NASM health document, III-6.
2. Ibid.

Section III: Preparing for Sunday

4. The nearer you are to the source of a sound, the greater the damage of hearing loss.

5. As the worship minister you are responsible for monitoring the decibel level of your sound system during a rehearsal or worship service. You need to establish a decibel level that your sound team will not exceed.

6. In order to monitor the levels of sound in your service, purchase a reliable decibel meter that can be installed at your soundboard so your technicians can monitor the levels throughout a rehearsal or service.

7. Also check the sound levels on the platform during a service. Monitors and amps can increase the sound level way beyond what is appropriate for you, your vocalists, and instrumentalists. Sometimes there is a terrible spiral that occurs as the singers ask for more volume in the monitors and the instrumentalists increase the level of their amps to compensate for the louder monitor levels. Train your worship team members to get by on less sound.

8. As the worship minister you need to be an advocate for good hearing health with your worship teams. Establish some policies for rehearsals and services and practice these policies.

9. Give your worship team a short break in a rehearsal to give their ears a time to rest. This is an ideal time to give a devotional thought.

In an effort to reduce platform sound levels the church where I serve began using in-ear monitors. The drummer is in a soundproof enclosure. Guitar amps are played at a very low level. There are no monitor speakers on the platform. Each person's in-ear monitor is individually adjusted to suit the singer or instrumentalist. As a result of going to in-ear monitors the level of sound on the platform dropped dramatically. We also had an easier time mixing the sound levels in the congregation since there was no "wash over" of sound from the platform monitors. In-ear monitors can be a great help, but the worship minister still needs to be on alert. If a worship team member is not careful, the in-ear monitor volume level can also be so high it can cause hearing damage.

If you plan on being an effective worship minister for many years, your physical health comes in a close second to your spiritual health. Be a good steward of the abilities the Lord has given you to use in service to his church. Make life-changing adjustments to the way you live through improving your diet, starting an exercise regimen, and getting enough sleep. Protect your vocal and hearing health through good behaviors that will help to ensure a lifetime of ministry.

SECTION IV

Discipling through Worship Ministry

CHAPTER 20

Discipling Your Worship Teams

How long will you be ministering at the church where you are currently serving? When you look back over three years or seven years or fifteen years, what will you accomplish for the kingdom of God at your place of ministry? None of us really knows how long the Lord will allow us to serve in a particular place. I remember a worship minister friend who went to serve as an interim worship minister for a short term and ended up serving at that church for eight years. Wherever the Lord leads us to serve, we should expect to be there for an extended time. We have to think long-term about investing in our place of ministry or else we may only do superficial things.

In addition to weekly worship planning and leading responsibilities, training disciples is a top priority for the worship minister. Training disciples takes priority over training musicians. Having a goal to help our worship teams improve their music skills is a good goal, but not as important a goal as helping those on our teams grow in their faith in Christ. We labor to provide the spiritual nourishment that our worship teams need weekly. Are your worship teams growing in their faith and walk with Christ?

Discipleship includes equipping. Our job is to not only to do ministry, but also to equip others to do ministry (Eph 4:12). We must invest in others, especially the younger generations who will one day be leaders in the church. What happens to the worship ministry at your church when you are no longer there? Does it dry up or flourish under the leadership of those you have mentored? Discipleship is an ongoing responsibility of the worship minister.

Section IV: Discipling through Worship Ministry

WHAT DID JESUS TELL US ABOUT TRAINING DISCIPLES?

One of the first places to look would be the Great Commission: "Go therefore and make disciples of all nations, baptizing them in the name of the Father and of the Son and the Holy Spirit, teaching them to observe all that I have commanded you. And behold, I am with you always, to the end of the age" (Matt 28:19–20). *Go*, *baptize*, and *teach* are the imperatives of Jesus in this passage. We also have a promise of the Lord's presence with us in the midst of this ministry. The focus of our ministry is where the Lord has planted us—the local church. As worship ministers we are surrounded by our worship teams in rehearsal and in our corporate worship services each week. These are people that God has put in our path to teach and equip.

We are supposed to teach everything that Jesus commands. How are we doing with our teams in teaching the commands of Christ? Are we teaching them to deny themselves and take up their cross and follow Christ (Matt 16:24–26)? Jesus uses crucifixion as the metaphor for being a disciple—denying self and embracing God's will no matter the cost.

As we teach the principles that Christ gave us, we also model this for our people. Jesus tells us that "a disciple is not above his teacher, but everyone when he is fully trained will be like his teacher" (Luke 6:40). It is a sobering thought to consider the influence we have with those in our worship ministry for the kingdom. Pastor Kevin DeYoung reminds us:

> The one indispensable requirement for producing godly, mature Christians is godly, mature Christians. Granted, good parents still have wayward children and faithful mentors don't always get through to their pupils. But in the church as a whole, the promise of 1 Peter 1 is as true as ever. If we are holy, we will be fruitful. Personal connections with growing Christians is what the next generation needs more than ever.[1]

How are you modeling what it is like to follow Christ?

Discipleship is "caught as much as it is taught." Collin Marshall and Tony Payne say, "We are always an example to those whom we are teaching and training, whether we like it or not. We cannot stop being an example. Are we modeling the way of the cross?"[2] We cannot lead our people to a spiritual place we have never been. The Apostle Paul instructed Timothy

---

1. DeYoung, "Reaching the Next Generation, Hold Them with Holiness."
2. Marshall and Payne, 74–75.

to "follow the pattern of sound words that you have heard from me, in the faith and love that are in Christ Jesus. By the Holy Spirit who dwells within us, guard the good deposit entrusted to you" (2 Tim 1:13–14). We want our lay people to follow our pattern of sound words that reflects the teachings of Scripture. This all the more reminds us of the daily necessity to be in the Word and spending time in prayer. We need the living water in order to give fresh rejuvenating living water to our people. This living water is the Holy Spirit working in and through us.

When we think of discipling our worship teams, we also must love those the Lord gives us to serve. Jesus said "a new commandment I give to you, that you love one another: just as I have loved you, you also are to love one another. By this all people will know that you are my disciples, if you have love for one another" (John 13:34–35). Do we care more about our team members than we do our program or our music? Not everyone on our teams is easy to love, yet we should love our people the way Christ loves them and loves us.

Discipling our worship teams includes mentoring small groups and one-on-one interaction. When you think about it, Jesus ministered to thousands of people, but called twelve disciples that he taught intensively. He also had an inner circle of three disciples (Peter, James, and John) with whom he invested beyond the times he spent with the twelve. David Kinnaman reminds us that "Disciples cannot be massed produced. They are handmade one relationship at a time."[3] Not only are we working in front of our groups week to week but we need to give focused attention to a few to mentor. This is especially important with younger generations in our ministries.

HOW DO WE DISCIPLE OUR TEAMS ON WEEKLY BASIS?

Each week at our rehearsals we are fighting a battle I call "the tyranny of the urgent." It is the week-in and week-out crunch of preparing our teams to lead music in the services. This urgency never lets up because Sunday is always coming. We also have the added challenge of preparing seasonal worship music with our teams and choirs along with the weekly worship music. So how do we carry out this important role of discipling?

How did Jesus model discipleship?

---

3. Kinnaman, *You Lost Me*, 10.

Section IV: Discipling through Worship Ministry

1. He called specific people with which to work.
2. He invested time daily and weekly. There was quantity and quality time.
3. He taught his disciples while on the way using everyday circumstances to make his points.
4. He taught them by example while in the midst of life's challenges.
5. He taught them privately.
6. He corrected his disciples when necessary.
7. He worked with them for an extended period of time.
8. He washed his disciples' feet, showing servant leadership with great humility.
9. He washed Judas's feet even when he knew Judas would betray him.

Jesus is our model when we seek to be intentional about discipleship with our worship teams. It is an investment of time day to day and week to week. We need to use the teachable moments in rehearsals as well as the moments before and after rehearsals. Sometimes we need to speak privately with a team member about a concern or listen to a team member who is having a difficult week. Being intentional about discipleship means building in some extra time before and after rehearsals and worship services to be available to people.

What are some other practical ways to disciple in the worship ministry setting? First, be purposeful about the music you choose for your teams to learn. Your worship team will remember a song text long after you quit using that particular song in worship. We want to give them a healthy theological song diet that is feeding them weekly. Why spend time learning songs that have vague meanings?

In the midst of a rehearsal setting take time to talk about the songs. We often talk to our teams about being expressive. This can be superficial unless they really understand the true meaning of the song and how it applies to their walk with Christ. We want them not simply reacting emotionally to a song but really understanding the objective truths in the song which grounds their expression.

We should plan a time at each rehearsal to read Scripture and pray. If we are not intentional about having a devotion time, it probably will not happen. You might want to pause in the middle of the rehearsal just for a few minutes to do this. Often if we wait until the end of the rehearsal, the time runs out and the devotion and prayer does not happen. When I am beginning a Sunday morning rehearsal in preparation for the worship service, many times I will do this devotion time first in order to get our heads and hearts ready for the task before us.

If you have a choir rehearsal each week, consider preparing a weekly rehearsal sheet that lists the songs you will rehearse in order and gives information about Sunday services. On a rehearsal sheet you can also put a short Scripture and devotional thought for your singers to read. I would take these rehearsal sheets and mail them to absentee members with a personal note from me. You can still send an email or text, but there is nothing like getting a letter in the mail with a personal note. You may even want to do a weekly email update to your worship teams that contains some spiritual food for the week.

It would be helpful two or three times a year to plan a rehearsal retreat on a Friday night or Saturday morning for your worship band or choir. At this rehearsal you can have an extended time to focus on new music and to spend some time "recharging the batteries" of your people with Scripture and prayer. I would often do this with the choir when they began learning Christmas music in the fall or when we restarted rehearsals in January. Having a guest speaker or clinician come to work with your group can also encourage them in their service on the worship team.

Are their members of your worship team with whom you could invest more individually? This could be a person who is struggling with some aspect of life or someone you want to encourage to consider ministry as a vocation. Of course men should only meet with other men and the same is true for women. One church where I served actually gave me a hospitality budget account to help pay for lunch meetings with church members or prospective church members.

If your church leadership is in favor, consider starting a worship internship program where each season or year you have a younger person work along side you in the worship ministry. This is a great way to provide training for someone who is considering worship ministry as a calling. It is helpful if there is a budget line item that can help pay expenses for the intern position. If not, it could always be a volunteer position.

In their book *The Trellis and the Vine*, Collin Marshall and Tony Payne present the concept of the church as a trellis and vine. The trellis (the structure of the church) makes it possible for the vine (the people) to

Section IV: Discipling through Worship Ministry

have growth in an organized and healthy way. The problem is that many churches become more focused on the structure (programs) than they are the people. Over the course of this discipleship-themed book the authors challenge the reader to think about how ministries should change:

- from running programs to building people,
- from running events to training people,
- from using people to growing people,
- from filling gaps to training new workers,
- from clinging to ordained ministry to developing team leadership, and
- from engaging in management to engaging in ministry.[4]

We must take a serious look at our worship ministries to insure we have an adequate structure in place, but our focus is to be on the people and their spiritual growth. As worship ministry leaders, we need to be intentional and sometimes creative in accomplishing an effective discipleship ministry among our worship teams. When you come to the end of your ministry will you see the fruit of years of faithful discipleship among your worship teams? Have you equipped others to continue the work after you are gone? Through training and equipping we work ourselves out of a job.

---

4. Marshall and Payne, *Trellis and the Vine*, 17–25.

CHAPTER 21

Discipling the Generations through Worship Ministry

UNLESS YOU SERVE IN a new church with mostly young adults or an older church made up of senior adults, you are probably serving in a multigenerational church. Most churches consist of a wide span of generations with a focus on discipling all ages. Today there is the possibility of six generations attending our worship services spanning one hundred years of the most phenomenal changes in history.[1] Churches should be concerned about all ages of people who attend their services and small group studies. How is the worship ministry on the local church level doing when it comes to ministering to the generations?

Sometimes churches choose to have two or more Sunday morning worship services, often with different music styles—classic and modern (or some other variation). Offering different styles of worship services tends to divide our congregations by generations. The older Christians rally around the more traditional service and younger generations attend the modern style service. There is definitely a loss factor for the church when the corporate worship time becomes segregated by age. This is not just a loss for older members but for the young members as well. Here are some thoughts on the generations from J. I. Packer, well-known theologian, author, and teacher:

> We have separated the ages, very much to the loss of each age. In the New Testament, the Christian church is an all-age community,

---

1 Menconi, *Intergenerational Church*, x.

> and in real life the experience of the family to look no further should convince us that the interaction of the ages is enriching. The principle is that generations should be mixed up in the church for the glory of God. That doesn't mean we shouldn't disciple groups of people of the same age or the same sex separately from time to time. That's a good thing to do. But for the most part, the right thing is the mixed community in which everybody is making the effort to understand and empathize with all the other people in the other age groups. Make the effort is the key phrase here. Older people tend not to make the effort to understand younger people, and younger people are actually encouraged not to make the effort to understand older people. That's a loss of a crucial Christian value in my judgment. If worship styles are so fixed that what's being offered fits the expectations, the hopes, even the prejudices, of any one of these groups as opposed to the others, I don't believe the worship style glorifies God, and some change, some reformation, some adjustment, and some enlargement of spiritual vision is really called for.[2]

Packer makes a good case for churches to strive for true intergenerational worship and to facilitate healthy communication among the generations in our churches.

Your largest multigenerational group appears on Sunday morning at the corporate worship time. Here you have children, teens, young adults, median adults, and senior adults present. As you plan the musical portion of the service each week you are preparing to minister to a wide range of ages. What considerations do you make for the different generations as you plan the service? In the church I serve I am mindful to not always sing the new songs. I select some quality hymns from years gone by that still have great impact today and will especially minister to the older ones in the midst. These hymns can be easily presented in an updated style.

How many generations are represented in your worship ministry? Churches who have worship choirs will often see several generations serving together. (This is another good reason to have a worship choir). Worship bands and teams tend to be made up of younger generations. A healthy worship ministry will have opportunities for all ages to participate and be discipled.

Although it may be difficult to involve several generations in the worship band, consider how you can involve more generations on the worship

---

2. Rosenthal, "Interview with J. I. Packer."

platform each Sunday. There are some among the older generations who have good instrumental skills that can be used on Sundays. Train younger generations to play instruments and sing in worship. Consider prayer and Scripture readings in the service given by senior adults or teenagers. Your Sunday morning platform should reflect the generations who attend your church.

In the Scripture there are many examples of the Lord using people of all ages for his kingdom work. The people of Israel were instructed in Deuteronomy 6 to be diligent to teach their children about the Lord at all times. The Lord used senior adult leaders such as Moses to do great work for him. Jesus always had time for children and saw the importance of the younger generations. Paul and Barnabus worked with young Mark in their missionary journeys, who although was initially immature later became a great leader in the church.

Consider the story of the boy Samuel and Eli the priest in 1 Samuel 3. Eli oversees the worship at the tent of meeting in Shiloh and Samuel is serving under Eli's leadership. One particular night as Samuel is sleeping in the worship area he hears a voice calling his name. Thinking it is Eli calling him, Samuel runs to Eli's side only to find out that Eli did not call his name. Samuel hears the voice two more times and runs to Eli. Finally, Eli perceives it is the Lord calling Samuel and instructs Samuel the next time he hears his name called to say, "Speak Lord, for your servant hears." When Samuel hears the voice the following time he answers and receives the Lord's instruction to him. The message Samuel heard was one of judgment on Eli and his sons.

Although the main purpose of this passage is focused on the calling of Samuel to be a prophet of the Lord and the judgment of the Lord on Eli and his sons, it is also an example of how this younger person needed an older person to sense the Lord's call in his life. We also see how God uses young people such as Samuel to carry his message to other generations. In our churches generations worshiping and serving together have great value for the body of Christ. Older Christians need to speak into the lives of younger Christians, helping them discern the Lord's leadership in their lives. Younger generations are used by God in our churches as well and need to be given opportunities to become leaders.

The worship ministry is suffering from a narrow vision when it is only concerned with one generation of church members and does not reach out to all generations. What can the worship minister do to promote

SECTION IV: DISCIPLING THROUGH WORSHIP MINISTRY

intergenerational worship ministry and equip the rising generations? In the chapters ahead we will attempt to address this question.

CHAPTER 22

Worship Ministry to Children

MOST CHURCHES ARE DILIGENT about teaching their children to follow Christ, but what are they doing to equip these children in worship ministry? One of the main goals of worship ministry is to equip and train leaders (see chapter 3). One of the best places to begin this equipping in our worship ministries is with our children. They are the future leaders in our churches. We first evangelize and equip them with the gospel. We then train in the area of music and worship. These passages remind us of the importance of this focus on children's worship ministry.

> These commandments that I give you today are to be upon your hearts. Impress them on your children. Talk about them when you sit at home and when you walk along the road, when you lie down and when you get up. (Deut 6:6–7)

> Train up a child in the way he should go, and when he is old he will not turn from it. (Prov 22:6)

> At that time the disciples came to Jesus, saying, "Who is the greatest in the kingdom of heaven?" And calling to him a child, he put him in the midst of them and said, "Truly, I say to you, unless you turn and become like children, you will never enter the kingdom of heaven. Whoever humbles himself like this child is the greatest in the kingdom of heaven. Whoever receives one such child in my name receives me, but whoever causes one of these little ones who believe in me to sin, it would be better for him to have a great millstone fastened around his neck and to be drowned in the depth of the sea." (Matt 18:1–5)

Section IV: Discipling through Worship Ministry

In his instructions in Deuteronomy Moses was fully aware of the urgency of passing down the faith to the children when he emphasized that parents were to teach their children about the Lord throughout the day. Proverbs reminds us how impressionable our children are at a young age to spiritual things and that principles taught in the early days follow them throughout their lives. Jesus teaches us the importance of repentance and coming to the kingdom with the attitude of a humble child. We also see the heavy weight of responsibility on the part of teachers working with children to be sure to not lead them in a direction away from the Lord.

The first place of teaching and modeling the gospel to our children is the home, but churches also have a responsibility in this training. Churches generally offer biblical instruction to children in age-graded groups on Sunday mornings. The worship ministry can also partner in this training by using music as a tool. One of the best ways to do this is through a children's choir ministry. Children's choirs often meet at church on Sunday nights or Wednesday nights depending on the church's weekly schedule. Why have a children's choir ministry?

DISCIPLESHIP

The primary reason to form a children's choir is for discipleship. As children's choir leaders work with children they are teaching the Gospel story, other Bible stories, worship principles, doctrines of the church, and the importance of sharing the faith (missions). Teaching about the Lord through the use of music is a wonderful way to help children remember great truths. Although some consideration needs to be given to the age of the children and their ability to understand biblical concepts, a well-chosen song to teach in children's choir can impact a child for life. People of all ages have a great way of remembering texts over long periods of time simply because these texts are set to music.

WORSHIP TRAINING

Children's choir ministry can function as an effective place to teach children about worship. Leaders can explain the biblical meaning of worship, share the importance of participating in worship, teach the great hymns of the faith, and show the role of music in worship. What better place to teach about worship than in a context where much of the rehearsal can be considered worship. How often are children helped to understand the meaning of worship in their daily lives and corporate gatherings? Children's choirs can also give opportunities for children to sing in worship as a group or individually.

MUSIC SKILL TRAINING

Children's choir ministry can equip children to read music. Children quickly learn to read musical notation through instruction and musical games. Since many schools are reducing their music training opportunities for children due to budget constraints, children's choir is a great place to continue this training. Because much of the focus in a children's choir ministry is on singing, leaders can effectively teach healthy vocal skills that will lead the child through a lifetime of singing. Children gain choral skills as they sing together in rehearsal and in the worship service. With the use of simple instruments a child can begin to learn how to play musical instruments in worship. Offering musical skill training to children begins a process of equipping children to participate on worship teams as they grow older.

OUTREACH

One of the best ways to reach children and their families who do not go to church is through a children's choir ministry. Many churches attract children from their community who desire to be involved with something musical by offering a children's choir ministry. A child may hear the gospel for the first time in a children's choir. The parents are reached when they bring the child and stay for a discipleship class or worship time for adults. Even if these parents just drop off their children for choir, they usually do attend the special worship programs of the church when the children sing. A children's choir ministry can also minister to the community when they share the gospel in a musical way at community events and places like retirement homes.

Discipleship, worship training, music skill training, and outreach are four great reasons the worship minister should implement a children's choir ministry at the church.

Section IV: Discipling through Worship Ministry

GETTING STARTED

If you decide to begin a children's worship ministry, where do you start? As mentioned earlier, any new ministry needs to be vetted with your pastor and leadership staff. The pastor needs to be "on board" with the idea and implementation of the children's choir ministry. If there is a children's ministry staff person, this person also needs to fully endorse the plan. Since it takes time to implement this kind of ministry, it is best to plan for a new children's choir ministry at least six to twelve months in advance.

The next two items to consider are time and space. When is the best time to offer children's choirs? The usual answer is when the church is already gathered together on a Sunday or Wednesday. The children's choir time works best when parents also have a Bible study or worship service to attend. The other issue to consider is what rooms at the church will be available for the children to use. Usually the children's Bible study rooms are the best rooms to use since they are already set up for children with kid-sized chairs and tables.

How many children's choirs will you begin? This will depend on the size of the church's children's ministry and the number of workers you can find to serve. If there are enough children and leaders, ideally three different choirs would be best: preschool (age 4–5), early elementary (grades 1–2), and older elementary (grades 3–5). This can vary according to the numbers of children at each age level. If you do not have enough children to divide into 3 groups, consider two groups (preschool and elementary age).

You must have an adequate number of workers for each children's choir. At least one of the adults needs to be someone who can lead the musical portion of the choir—someone who enjoys singing and has some musical background. This person need not have a college music degree to lead, but any amount of musical training will help. Other helpers in the room can assist with discipline and minor things that come up in the rehearsal. As a rule there can be no less than two adult workers in each choir rehearsal. This is a liability issue but also makes common sense. Depending on the number of children in each choir, match a proportionate number of adults. Younger children generally need more supervision.

These workers need to be trained to know what to do in a children's choir rehearsal. If you do not help your children's choir leaders get equipped, they can become discouraged and burn out quickly. If you have experience with children's choir ministry, you can provide the training. If not, consider bringing in an expert in the area who can do some training. You might also check for online resources that will help equip your workers.

Once you round up support for a new children's choir ministry, discover a good place and time to meet, and train a number of workers, the next step is to promote the children's choir ministry. Work through the already existing children's ministry to reach out to children and parents at your church. Be creative in getting the word out about the new children's choir ministry. No publicity substitutes for personal invitations to children and parents to participate. Use the summer Vacation Bible School as a place to advertise the upcoming children's choir program in the fall. Consider having a fun afternoon or night promotional activity on a Friday or Saturday for children that promotes the new children's choir. When you set a date for the first night of the choir, make sure you do not wait too long after the first day of school. Sometimes worship ministers will wait until after Labor Day weekend to begin the children's choir ministry when school has already been in session for at least three weeks. Every child's activity or sport is vying for their time. The children's choir ministry needs to start early enough to involve the children before their schedules are full.

WHAT TO DO IN CASE OF A CHILDREN'S CHOIR REHEARSAL

Here are several general principles to consider when planning a children's choir rehearsal.

1. The adult leaders need to arrive early and well prepared for the rehearsal. Once the children arrive there is no time to be organizing materials or setting up the space. You will lose control of the rehearsal if you are not prepared by the time the first child steps into your room.

2. Plan early arriver activities for children who appear before the designated time. This happens regularly, especially when they are coming from a Wednesday supper at the church.

3. Plan more activities for a rehearsal than you need. Sometimes an activity you think will take fifteen minutes may be finished in five minute, or the activity you planned may not be working well and you need to move on to another one.

4. Plan a fast-paced rehearsal. You need to consider the attention spans of the children in your choir; the younger the age, the shorter the attention span. When you move from one activity to the next, make sure you do this immediately with no breaks. Discipline problems happen when you pause.

5. Remember that the children need to move. This is not the same as your adult worship choir who are comfortably seated for ninety minutes while you lead the rehearsal. Children need to move with the music. Plan some choreography or sign language for them to do as they sing. Younger children should march to the music or do some kind of music game that involves music. Use movement as another avenue of teaching.

6. Make your rehearsal fun. Most of the children have been sitting in a school classroom all day and do not look forward to another forty-five to sixty minutes of a school-like meeting. Remember that children elect to come to choir whereas they must go to school. You can make the rehearsal fun and teach great principles without them even knowing they are learning.

7. Look for music that gives great clarity to the meaning of the gospel and other biblical principles. Our first goal is discipleship and this requires great songs. These songs also need to be in a range to fit the child's voice. Younger children need simpler songs due to where they are developmentally. Hymns are great to teach to older children but preschoolers and children in grades 1 and 2 may struggle with the number of words in a hymn and the complexity of some of the concepts.

8. If you are the director of the choir, make sure you have helpers in the room that can deal with discipline issues as you lead. If you have to stop a rehearsal to correct a child, you may lose all forward momentum of the rehearsal.

9. Pray for your children before you arrive and pray with your children at the rehearsal. Keep in mind that your first goal of the rehearsal is discipleship, followed by worship training and music skill training. Care for their souls. Make sure you model Christ and talk about Christ.

10. Begin and end your rehearsal on time. Always begin on time no matter how many children are present. If you routinely wait for more children to appear before starting, children will begin coming late on purpose knowing that the rehearsal does not usually start on time.

RESOURCES

Finding songs and music resources for children's choir can be an adventure. There are several organizations that regularly publish children's choir materials (LifeWay, Sovereign Grace Music, Choristers Guild, Growing in Grace, and others). Several Christian music publishers regularly make available new children's choir musicals. You may want to pull together your own children's choir curriculum. Consider using worship songs that are current in the services at your church to teach the children. Introduce new songs to the children that will be used in future worship services. Select nine hymns you want to teach the children during the fall and spring and teach a new hymn each month.

What are some alternative ways of accomplishing the goals for a children's worship ministry if there is no children's choir at your church?

MUSIC ACADEMY

Another way a church can accomplish some of these same goals is to begin a music academy. The music academy offers private or group music lessons to children, teens, and adults. Through the academy students receive instruction on many different instruments and voice. The worship minister or another designated person at the church sets the guidelines for the academy and administrates the ministry. Music teachers are interviewed and invited to teach private or group lessons at the church during the week. One of the main stipulations for these music teachers is church membership at your church or active involvement in another evangelical church. So much of private lesson instruction is a matter of the modeling Christ to the students, so a church should use music teachers who love the Lord and enjoy working with children.

A number of years ago I was at a conference and heard an older worship pastor sharing about his church's music academy. He was a long-time worship pastor at a large evangelical church. Each year when the church would have its seasonal worship music programs at Christmas, Easter, and other times in the year, he would invariably have to hire a number of instrumentalists to supplement the church orchestra. This worship pastor always prayed that the Lord would send instrumentalists to his church. After a while the Lord impressed on him that this was the wrong prayer. The worship ministry should be training a generation of instrumentalists to serve the Lord in that church. This was the beginning of a fruitful time of training children and others musically through a newly established music academy. It took several years but the goal of raising up musicians to serve in the worship ministry was accomplished. Many of the adults who now serve in the worship ministry at the church began their musical training in the church's music academy.

SUMMER MUSIC DAY CAMP

A worship ministry can accomplish the goals of discipleship, worship training, music skill training, and outreach by offering a week-long music day camp in the summer. There are a couple of different approaches to this day camp. One approach is to offer musical experiences in small groups and a large group. In the small group times children can choose from a variety of activities, such as learning an instrument like a recorder, handbells, or guitar. The small group time can also feature learning sign language to a worship song, drama skits, or music games. At the large group time, the children come together to sing in a choir.

Another possible way to do a summer music camp is to learn a children's musical in a week. This is accomplished through early registration a couple of months in advance when each child receives a recording of the musical. Drama and solo auditions are held a few weeks prior to the day camp. The week of the camp the leader polishes the vocal parts of each song with the children, working on solos and drama parts and staging the musical. Children learn fast and when they have a recording of the musical early they arrive with the songs fairly well learned.

Consider offering afternoon recreation as part of your music day camp. Some music day camps may run from 9:00 a.m. to noon. When we offered our music day camp it would run to 3:00 p.m. each day and include some fun activities. The children would bring their own lunches. The afternoon recreation for the week would include bowling, skating, miniature golf, and water games. We would usually finish at noon on Friday and then offer the musical worship program that evening for parents. When we offered the final worship program on Sunday night, we found that sometimes parents would elect to start their vacations and leave town on Saturday. This would mean several children would miss the final worship service. It was not uncommon for us to have one hundred children involved in our summer day camp, which required a large number of parent and teen helpers to facilitate.

The summer day camp idea needs to be coordinated with the children's ministry summer activities and children's leadership at the church. If my church offered Vacation Bible School in June, I would schedule the music day camp for a week in July. Parents are looking for meaningful activities for their children to do in the summer and the music day camp is usually well attended by the church children and others from the community. If your church does not have a children's choir ministry, you could use the summer music day camp as a catalyst to get one started in the fall.

A children's choir ministry is a wonderful way to impact a younger generation in your church with the gospel. Using music to disciple children is a great tool for teaching spiritual truth that will last a lifetime. The children's choir ministry is the front end of the worship ministry equipping goal: training the next generation to love Jesus and be expressive in worship.

CHAPTER 23

Worship Ministry to Students

STUDENT MINISTRY IN THE church should be a top priority. Parents, of course, should be the front line of discipleship training with their middle school and high school children, but the church must come alongside to help in this training. This is especially true for the students who do not come from homes that have a positive Christian influence. The cultural voices today seem so loud through the many prevailing media sources that our students can be easily confused or led astray. A strong Bible-based student ministry is more vital today than at any other time in the life of the church.

I am certainly grateful for the influence the student ministry of my church had in my life as a young Christian. I first considered a call to ministry in my local church youth group and was blessed to have many worship ministry opportunities. Not only should churches bring focus on discipleship training with students, but we should also be using these years to train them in worship ministry. Where I teach many of the college-level men and women studying worship received formative training when they sang in their student choirs, led worship, or played in the worship bands in their local church student ministries. Worship ministry with students is an investment both in the students' lives and for the future of worship ministry in the church.

Churches that do children's choir ministry well often do not have training opportunities for these children when they reach their middle school and high school years. What is the cause of this lack of opportunity for this age group in our churches? I think there are several root causes that include:

1. The student minister at the church does not value worship ministry training for the students. Many student ministers perhaps did not experience opportunities for training in worship ministry when in their teen years and therefore do not see the value for it in the ministries they now lead.
2. The worship minister does not make this age group a priority in worship training.
3. The students may view musical groups as not "cool" and elect not to get involved.
4. Worship ministry training is not a primary concern because of the already limited time given for student ministry activities. Today students' schedules are crowded due to school and extra curricular activities, leaving less time for student ministry opportunities.
5. There may be few students who have the musical skills to serve on a worship team if there was no children's choir ministry in the church preparing these students.

Why have worship ministry opportunities for middle school and high school students? As stated earlier, one of the primary tasks of the worship ministry in the church is to equip people for ministry, and what better generation of Christians to equip than those in our student ministry. We sometimes fail to see what a wonderful discipleship tool is available through the use of musical worship experiences with this age group. Helping students learn the truths of God's Word through the use of songs can fuel discipleship in the student ministry. Teaching students the biblical principles of worship through their involvement in worship bands or ensembles directly impacts congregational worship now and for years to come. Using worship ministry teams to assist in mission outreach opens doors for the students to minister in places that may previously have been closed to the gospel. There are some great reasons to include worship ministry opportunities in the student ministry of the church. I know because student worship ministry changed the direction of my life as a teen and certainly influenced my call to ministry.

SECTION IV: DISCIPLING THROUGH WORSHIP MINISTRY

STARTING A STUDENT WORSHIP MINISTRY

If your church does not currently have any worship teams for teens, here are some principles to consider as you get started.

1. Your pastor should be first to approve of a new worship ministry team. Make sure he is "on board" with plans to work with this age group in worship ministry.
2. If your church has a student minister, this person should be fully supportive of the plan. Your student minister is ultimately responsible for the weekly student ministry schedule and needs to approve the rehearsal times for student worship teams.
3. As the worship minister, find out how to be involved in the student ministry of your church and meet the students and leaders.
4. Discover what students have vocal and instrumental skills. Ask students if they are involved in music groups at school such as choir, band, or orchestra. These particular students may become your beginning worship team members.
5. Decide what type of worship team would be best for the students at your church. Do you have a number of interested singers? Are there students who could play instruments in a worship band?
6. Determine resources you will need to lead the worship ministry, such as instruments, sound equipment, and amps.
7. Plan for the budget needs of student worship teams.
8. In conjunction with the student ministry, plan a calendar of worship ministry opportunities for a year.

POSSIBLE STUDENT WORSHIP TEAMS: THE STUDENT CHOIR

The traditional way of investing in students in worship ministry has been through the use of a choir. For many years the church youth choir was at the center of the student ministry. A number of churches still have student choirs today. Choirs in general have been on the decline in our churches due to the newer styles of worship services; however, I believe a student choir can still have a vital place in worship ministry today. Choirs can easily accommodate many more participants than a worship band. Inevitably there seems to be more singers wanting to participate in worship ministry than instrumentalists.

In some churches choirs are making a comeback even in worship settings that are ultra modern in style. This can work in a student setting also. The best way to build a student choir is from the ground up. Build an effective children's choir ministry first and then promote those children into the student choir when they reach their middle school years. It takes years to build a student worship ministry. You may need to add a middle school choir first and later a high school choir as your students mature. When you consider this the question may very well be, "Do you have the patience and perseverance to build a student choir or worship band ministry?"

SUGGESTIONS FOR EFFECTIVE STUDENT CHOIR REHEARSALS:

1. Don't go into a rehearsal without a well-thought-out rehearsal plan.
2. Sing music that the students enjoy singing (you can find great lyrics set in a modern style). Later you can introduce other music that may give them more challenge.
3. Make your rehearsal fast paced and fun. Strive for a rehearsal time that is enjoyable, but get some work done. Work on your humor.
4. Sing more and talk less. The students came to sing so let them sing. This also helps with disruptions and discipline issues.
5. Do not single out students and embarrass them when it comes to their vocal skills. Do group things and section things. Many students are self-conscious at this age, especially when it comes to their voices and fitting in the group.
6. Make sure you are pointing to the gospel message in your songs, devotion time, and prayers.
7. Always arrive early and be ready to start the rehearsal on time. This also gives you time to talk with the students as they arrive.
8. Start and end strong. Do songs they can sing well at the beginning and end of the rehearsal. Let them leave knowing that they were successful as a worship team.

9. Provide opportunities for the choir to sing in worship. You will lose your singers if they always practice but never get to share in the service.

10. Help the students understand the purpose for the student choir as leaders in worship and restate the purpose often. As the leader you must cast the vision.

THE STUDENT WORSHIP BAND

Another great avenue for worship ministry to students is through the use of a student worship band. This group of students can minister in the student gatherings at the church and occasionally in the corporate worship times of the church. The success of a worship band depends on the availability of students who can play worship band instruments. Some churches are blessed with students who have these skills. Others may need to provide training in order to prepare some student worship band members. If your church needs instrumentalists, find some skilled teachers in the area who are willing to work with your students. Perhaps the worship ministry budget could help fund some of these lesson times in order to train students for the worship band. Consider using some adult worship band members at your church to mentor these younger players.

If you have enough student instrumentalists, you could form more than one worship band and rotate the bands in worship settings. This gives more students the possibility of participation. You might also consider having a younger worship band and an older one. Or you could have a training band and a main band for the worship times. There are many possibilities but what works in your church setting depends on the make up of your student ministry.

Other considerations for student worship bands:

1. Follow many of the same principles mentioned in the student choir rehearsal suggestions above.

2. Disciple your band spiritually and help them grow musically.

3. Encourage private lessons on their instruments.

4. Stress the importance of dependability and punctuality with the members. There is only one person per instrument or just a few vocalists so each person is vital to the group.

5. If you have a student choir, let the worship band learn the music for the choir and accompany them in the worship service.
6. Have experts come in and work with the band. They may say the same things you say as the director but they are the "experts" and can reinforce things you are teaching the students.

STUDENT ENSEMBLES

If you do not have enough singers to make a choir, consider smaller worship ensembles such as a small group of your student ministry girls, boys, or a small three- or four-part group of girls and boys. These ensembles could provide vocal leadership with a Sunday morning worship band or work up songs to sing alone in the service. If you want to eventually have a student choir and you do not have the number of students needed, start with the smaller ensemble.

OTHER POSSIBLE WAYS TO DO STUDENT WORSHIP MINISTRY:

- Private lessons on an instrument through a church music academy
- Short-term student worship ministry teams for special events
- Worship ministry teams formed to help on student mission trips
- Students serving with adult worship ministry teams or choir
- Students who play band or orchestral instruments invited to play with adult worship teams or provide music for the prelude or offertory
- Summer student worship ministry camp—week-long day camp for a student worship band or choir
- Student worship ministry overnight retreats for team building and rehearsal
- Mentoring a student who shows aptitude in worship ministry

If you have a student worship team, consider implementing similar discipleship practices as mentioned earlier in discussions about the main worship team at the church. Once again, choosing worship songs that have good theological content is vital in your goal to disciple your students. The

Section IV: Discipling through Worship Ministry

lyrics help them throughout the week when walking with Christ is difficult at school, work, or home. Take time in rehearsals to read Scripture and pray with your students.

As the leader of a student worship team, you will need to decide upon rules and standards for your student teams. Here are some questions to consider for effective student worship teams:

1. Who can sing in the choir or play in the worship band? Does a student need to be a Christian to participate? Does a student need to be a member of the church? Students who are professing Christians should be the standard for participation on a worship team.

2. Can a student sing in the choir or play in the worship band at a worship service if they missed the previous rehearsal?

3. What is the dress code for rehearsals and leading worship? This needs to be addressed early to prevent situations arising when a student arrives with questionable clothing.

4. When your choir or band is preparing for a special service that requires several rehearsals in which to prepare, how many rehearsals can a student miss and still participate? It can be demoralizing for students who make most of the rehearsals to have a student show up at the last rehearsal and still participate in the program.

5. What actions can cause a student to be asked to leave a student worship team?

The success of the student worship ministry depends on a good partnership with the student minister. When deciding calendar worship events that involve the students, it is essential to align these well with the main student ministry calendar. This partnership involves two-way communication between you and the student minister. Invite the student minister to drop in on rehearsals and pray for the students. Include the student minister in worship ministry events. It would be good for you to attend some student ministry events that have nothing to do with the worship ministry. This builds strong connections with the student minister and gives you the opportunity to get to know the students outside of rehearsals.

When planning and implementing student worship ministry events or worship times, you want to keep not only the student minister informed but also the parents of the students. For the younger students their parents provide the primary transportation to these events. Communication with the parents is just as important as communication with the students. The parents can be strong advocates for the student worship ministry team if they feel they are connected.

How will your church use worship ministry to disciple your middle school and high school students? There is more than one way to do this. The important principle is that there is worship ministry training provided to this generation of people at your church. Churches that have a children's choir ministry and then no particular training in worship until the adult age group are missing kingdom opportunities with student worship ministry. Sometimes accomplishing student worship ministry training requires the worship minister to think outside of the box. When you provide student worship ministry at your church, you could be training the next worship leader, choir member, instrumentalist, or congregational singer for your church or someone else's church. You could provide the opportunity for the Spirit to change a student's life eternally.

CHAPTER 24

The Worship Choir

WHEN CONSIDERING THE USE of a worship choir, we see a number of places in Old Testament worship where the Levite choir served in worship. Fifty-five of the Psalms list instructions for the choir director. Choirs played a major role in the worship life of Israel, especially in King David's time. Although there is no mention of choirs in the New Testament, except perhaps the worship scenes around the throne in Revelation, choirs can have an important role in worship today.

Some maintain that since there is no mention of choirs in the New Testament we should not have choirs in worship today. The New Testament is also silent on a number of other worship issues, such as the correct order of a worship service, whether or not to use of instruments for congregational singing, and how often we should practice the Lord's Supper. Choirs were a part of Old Testament worship and the New Testament does not forbid choirs. For hundreds of years the choir played a role in congregational worship in churches around the world. Not every church needs to have a choir, but a worship choir can certainly be effective in worship ministry today.

Perhaps some of the hesitation for using choirs in worship today has to do with the idea that choirs are performing for the congregation. In some worship ministries the choir performance model is present. Helping the choir see that their role is not to entertain but to lead and encourage the congregation is the responsibility of the worship minister week to week. I do believe that the largest choir in our worship services is the congregation and that congregational singing is the primary way we should use music in our services. There is also a place for the choir to sing alone in the service

The Worship Choir

as they edify and encourage the congregation. When you think about it, in our worship services we have people come to the platform to pray, read Scripture, or give a testimony. Why is it different when the choir sings a song that is a prayer, a Scripture text, or a testimony?

In a sermon on Ephesians 5:17–20 pastor John Piper shared this thought about choirs:

> Singing is to be to each other. [Ephesians 5] Verse 19 says "speaking to one another in psalms, hymns and spiritual songs, singing and making melody with your heart to the Lord." Here is the clearest mandate for corporate worship in the New Testament. You can't obey this in solitude. God calls us to speak in song to one another. . . the use of solos or musical groupings like worship teams and choirs can be part of this speaking to one another in songs. If it is good to speak to each other in songs as we do this in a Godward way, then we don't always have to do it all at the same time, though we do think that congregational singing should be the defining sound of our worship. A choir can speak the Word to us in song from the heart, filled with the Spirit, with a view to God's presence and undergirded by a deep, biblical theology of God's sovereign goodness. And we can hear this and say Yes and Amen to the glory of God.[1]

Choirs have an edifying role in the worship service, but there are a number of reasons churches may not have a choir. Some churches do not have choirs today because their platform space is not large enough to accommodate a choir. Other churches that meet in a temporary worship space may have nowhere for a choir to rehearse during the week. Some worship leaders today do not have the training needed to work with a choir or do not see the value of a choir ministry. There may be some thought that a choir cannot work in a more modern-style worship setting. I have found that choirs can adapt well to many different musical styles of worship.

So, why have a worship choir? When a worship choir is trained to be leaders in worship, they bring great energy and involvement in the worship service. The worship choir at my church does not sing every week but when they do sing it can be quite powerful. When we have a worship band, praise singers, and a large choir on risers singing praise to the Lord, it is such an encouragement and example to your congregation. Having an expressive group of singers supporting the congregational singing is also a great support to the worship leader.

1. Piper, "Singing and Making Melody to the Lord."

Section IV: Discipling through Worship Ministry

A worship choir can introduce new songs to your congregation. I use this method to help the congregation hear a new song before they have to sing it. The choir can take several weeks in rehearsal to prepare a song and effectively teach the song to the congregation. We often introduce new songs during the time in the service when we are taking the offering.

While a worship band and praise team may consist of ten members, a choir can be much larger. There are probably a number of people in your congregation who do not fit the requirements of the worship band or praise team, but they could sing in the choir. The choir gives an opportunity for more people to serve in worship ministry. Having a choir also gives the worship minister a larger group of worship team members to disciple. The larger the worship ministry, the more influence you can have for the kingdom as you minister in the lives of your people. The worship choir can function as another small group ministry of your church giving opportunities for discipleship and fellowship.

The worship choir is often the one place in the worship ministry that is intergenerational. It is a picture for the church of several generations coming together to worship the Lord. Most worship choirs are open to eighteen-year-olds through senior adults. Some churches may also include high school students in the choir. The worship choir provides life-long opportunities for people to serve the Lord. There is a gentleman in my worship choir who has been a member of the choir for fifty years.

Another reason to use a worship choir is the musical diversity it can bring to the service. The worship band can be somewhat limited on style, but the worship choir can give a musical offering that can be a fresh expression to the Lord. Sometimes the choir at my church will sing an a cappella song or sing only using piano accompaniment. The choir could sing a worship song from a different era that helps us stay rooted to our heritage as the church.

The worship minister should strive weekly to raise the musical and vocal skills of the worship choir through instruction in the rehearsal. Over a period of time this can raise the musical excellence of the worship services.

There are many great reasons to have a worship choir actively involved in the worship ministry of the church. It is an investment in the lives of some dear church members and a great encouragement to your congregation.

The Worship Choir

SOME CONSIDERATIONS ON THE CARE AND FEEDING OF THE WORSHIP CHOIR

1. Even though the worship choir's main responsibility is to encourage congregational singing, they also need to have the challenge of working on some songs that they will share in the service. It is difficult to motivate a choir whose only responsibility is singing with the congregation.

2. A worship choir can be helpful with seasonal music at Christmas or Easter. Many churches would like to hear traditional and new songs associated with the seasons. It is common to begin work on Christmas music in late August and Easter music in January.

3. Unless you are serving in a church that is accustomed to having the choir sing every week, consider using the choir once or twice a month on Sunday mornings. This helps to keep the weekly rehearsal time less pressured and gives more time for the choir to prepare music. It also allows for time in the rehearsal to prepare seasonal music.

4. Give the choir breaks during the year. Many choirs will be off several weeks after Christmas and sometimes a month to six weeks in the summer. This allows your singers a chance to rest and look forward to when the choir rehearsals resume.

5. Conduct your choir like another small group ministry. Keep attendance records so you can remember who was present. Take time to share some Scripture and pray with your people at each rehearsal. Be pastoral with your people.

6. Look for choir music that is accessible for your singers but also gives them some musical challenge. It is good not to discourage the choir with music that is too difficult for them but a choir can be bored with music that does not push them some. Find a balance for your singers. They will not grow musically if there is not some challenge to the music.

7. Implement a dress code for the choir (and worship team). Don't wait for something to happen that is difficult to handle. Choir robes take care of most of the dress code issues, but in the last few years robes have been eliminated in many churches.

SECTION IV: DISCIPLING THROUGH WORSHIP MINISTRY

8. Select lay leaders in the choir who can help with details such as getting choir music in folders, storing music, taking attendance, greeting choir members, and helping new members get acclimated.

9. Plan to work on several songs at the weekly rehearsal. Know what songs you will use in worship for the next couple of months and work ahead on these songs with the choir. It is difficult for the choir member to spend a half hour or an hour of a rehearsal on just one or two songs. Each week the rehearsal should consist of songs that will be sung in church over the next six weeks.

10. As director, go into your rehearsal with a plan. Start and end on time. Work fast and don't talk too much. Begin and end your rehearsal with familiar songs. Work the songs for Sunday worship toward the middle of the rehearsal so late arrivers are present for them.

11. Strive to keep the rehearsal space comfortable and uncluttered. Be sure the piano is tuned regularly. It is difficult to sing well with a piano that is out of tune.

12. Just as you would with your worship band, decide in advance who can serve in the choir. Do they need to be church members? What age singers are invited?

13. Provide some training opportunities for the choir occasionally when you invite another choir leader to work with your singers or give them an inspirational message to encourage them in their service to the church.

14. Consider having a rehearsal retreat at the church on a Friday or Saturday to work on seasonal music or to get a head start on the music for the next several months.

15. Decide on some fellowship events for the choir where choir members can get to know each other outside of the normal rehearsal time.

If your church does not currently have a worship choir, consider starting one. Implementing a seasonal choir that will function for a few weeks and sing for Christmas or Easter services is a great way to see the response of possible choir members and the congregation towards a choir. If the seasonal choir works well, consider stretching the time the choir meets for fall and spring. Choosing great worship songs, inspiring the choir to lead in worship, discipling them as they rehearse, and providing pastoral care for them will keep choir members coming back to rehearsal week after week.

CHAPTER 25

Worship Ministry to Senior Adults

And now behold, the Lord has kept me alive, just as he said, these forty-five years since the time the Lord spoke to Moses, while Israel walked in the wilderness. And now behold, I am this day eighty-five years old. I am strong today as I was in the day that Moses sent me; my strength now is as my strength then, for war and for going and coming. So now give me this hill country of which the Lord spoke on that day, for you heard how the Anakim were there, with great fortified cities. It may be that the Lord will be with me, and I shall drive them out just as the Lord said.
Joshua 14:10–12.

Wisdom is with the aged, and understanding in length of days.
Job 12:12

So even to old age and gray hairs, O God, do not forsake me, until I proclaim your might to another generation, your power to all those to come.
Psalms 71:18

So we do not lose heart. Though our outer self is wasting away, our inner self is being renewed day by day.
2 Corinthians 4:16

A number of years ago I was interviewing with a church for a worship pastor position. This would be my third full-time worship ministry position. In the first two churches my responsibilities were in the areas of

Section IV: Discipling through Worship Ministry

worship and student ministry. I was fairly well acclimated to the worship and student ministry combination. Although I treasured the time in those early years of working with students, my primary training and gifting was in worship ministry. As my family grew with the birth of our first child, I soon determined that the combination position of worship and student ministry was taking a toll on my home life. I decided that if the Lord were to move me to another church I would pray that the responsibilities would only be in the worship area. In the discussion with this third church they asked if I could provide some oversight to an already existing, lay-led senior adult ministry. I immediately thought about my concern of accepting another combination ministry position. The worship minister search team assured me that the senior adult ministry work would be 10 percent of my overall responsibilities at the church. Having had no training in working with senior adults, I accepted the call to that church to serve as their worship and senior adult minister. I was grateful that this church already had a well-established senior adult ministry with senior adult leaders who enthusiastically led the ministry. They mainly wanted me to assist in calendar planning, represent the senior adults in church staff meetings, and travel with them on trips several times a year.

One of my immediate discoveries working with this group is that they arrive very early for meetings and events. I was accustomed to arriving a few minutes early for student ministry activities and being the first one present. At the senior adult activities I was usually the last one to arrive even though I was actually on time. I discovered that senior adults like to eat out at nice restaurants not fast-food places and that they often paid for my meal. They would stop by my office during the week as they volunteered time at the church and bring me snacks and gifts. When we traveled overnight they went to their hotel rooms early and were up early for breakfast. I did not have to stay up checking to see if they were wandering around the hotel late at night as I did with the students. When we finished a trip or event they were always grateful and made a point to tell me how much they appreciated me. I quickly decided that senior adult ministry was very different from student ministry in a good way. I loved working with students but I grew to love working with senior adults just as much.

Senior adults at your church may have been church members for many years. We recently had a church member pass away that was a member at my church for eighty years. Senior adults invest their time and their money in the church. A great percentage of the giving at multigenerational churches usually comes from the senior adult age group. Senior adults are often looking for opportunities to serve and mentor younger generations at church. As Christians age their roles may change at work and at church, but they do not retire from serving the Lord. Senior adults can have a vital role in the life of the church and should be encouraged to serve and be given places to serve in the church.

What are some ways senior adults can serve in the worship ministry?

1. Many are capable of being involved in your Sunday morning choirs, praise teams, and instrumental groups.
2. Many have time to volunteer during the week to assist with setup, cleanup, and other administrative duties in the worship ministry.
3. Many can assist in the children's choir ministry.
4. Many can be excellent helpers for music day camps or other children's music activities.
5. Many could serve in a senior adult choir.

If you don't have a senior adult choir, consider starting one. Although some of your senior adults may sing in the main worship choir, there could also be a choir for senior adults. A senior adult choir can give you opportunities to get to know this age group and minister to them. It can also be an outreach arm for the church as they sing in retirement homes and other places in the city. Senior adults also enjoy a choir such as this just for the opportunity to fellowship. Many of them live alone and the highlight of their day is to join with fellow brothers and sisters in Christ to sing.

Here are some considerations when working with a senior adult choir.

1. Decide on a convenient time for the choir to meet. The best time to meet is during the day since many senior adults do not like to drive in the evening.
2. Use a good rehearsal space that is easily assessable to senior adults.
3. Find an accompanist who can meet for a daytime rehearsal and who loves being around senior adults. Perhaps there is a senior adult who has the piano skill to accompany the group.
4. Look for worship music that is assessable to senior adults. Songs should be in a comfortable range and not rhythmically challenging. Look for arrangements of some of their favorite hymns or create some of your own hymn arrangements.

5. Schedule times the choir can sing. The choir will find it tiring to rehearse and not have opportunities to share the songs with others. Consider retirement homes in the area as possible outreach places. If your church has a Wednesday night or Sunday night service, plan times for the choir to share in these services. Plan on at least one opportunity to sing either at the church or a retirement center each month.

6. Make the choir rehearsal an enjoyable experience and something the senior adults look forward to attending each week.

7. Gauge the difficulty of the arrangements for the members who attend. It could be that a few read music and most do not. There is nothing wrong with doing simple hymn arrangements.

Having a senior adult choir creates discipleship and pastoral opportunities for the worship minister. In the midst of preparing the music never lose sight of the need to make the gospel clear to this age group. It is easy to assume that these men and women are spiritually mature and do not need to hear Scripture or an encouraging gospel word. They need to hear this word as much as any other generation in the church.

When I involve senior adults in the worship ministry, I discover that they often become my strongest supporters. They may not always agree with the music style of the service, but they grow to love you and what you are trying to do in the worship ministry. Finding opportunities to involve senior adults builds bridges with the oldest generation in the church and connects them to other generations in your worship ministry.

How encouraging is your worship ministry to senior adults? Your worship ministry should mirror the generations in your church. How much effort do you make as a worship minister to see the generations come together in the worship ministry?

CHAPTER 26

Safeguarding the Worship Ministry

WORSHIP MINISTERS SHOULD BE on the offensive to provide a safe environment for those in their care whether they are working with children, students, or adults. There are a number of considerations that go into the day-to-day work, rehearsals, and special events of the worship ministry. Some occurrences may be outside of your control but many can be prevented through careful planning and a watchful eye.

WORSHIP MINISTRY WITH CHILDREN AND STUDENTS

The world we live in today has changed. Things that my parents allowed me to do as a child, I would never consider letting my children do today for their safety in our society. The same should be true for children in our church. Here are some principles to put into action in the worship ministry.

1. Your church should have a policy concerning who can serve in the preschool, children's, or student ministries. Many churches require a person to be a member of the church for at least a year before beginning to serve in these areas. Sometimes the problem that occurs with this policy is that a church may be desperate for workers and forgo this rule. It is the shortcuts that will open the ministry to trouble.

2. All workers with children must be screened in advance. Churches should run a background check to see if people desiring to serve in the children's or student ministry have past records that would prevent them from serving. For potential workers who want to serve and have

been members for a short time, consider checking with their former church for a reference. Due diligence to discover past behaviors of the worker is extremely important.

3. Your church should decide what age of worker can supervise preschoolers, children, or students. It is not uncommon for a teenage girl or boy to be asked to serve with preschoolers or children in lieu of an adult because there are not enough adults to fill the positions. Teenagers should not take the place of adult workers but they can work along side adults in these areas.

4. When working with preschoolers, children, or students, the church must adopt the two-worker rule. At no time should an adult be alone with a child while at children's events (rehearsals, Bible studies, activities, restroom breaks). When working with children at church there must be enough adults serving so that at no time is a worker left alone with a child. This principle keeps accountability both for the adult and the child. Even if the adult does nothing wrong, a child can falsely accuse the adult of a certain behavior.

5. It is important to get to know the parents of the children in your ministry. Understanding some of the home dynamics can help prepare you for potential issues. Many children live in a one-parent home. Discover who is allowed to pick up the students after a rehearsal or activity. It could be that a parent or relative who is not allowed to pick up a child could attempt to do so after an event.

6. Your church should have a check-in and check-out system in place to keep track of the children who are participating in an activity. Many churches use software-based systems that track attendance and can also create nametags for the children. The younger the child, the more supervision that is needed for arrival and pick-up times.

7. It is necessary to keep good records on each child or student in your worship ministry, including emergency contact information. Taking roll at each rehearsal or event will help you keep track of which members have missed for a week or more. As the ministry to the children or students grows, it becomes difficult to remember who was in attendance without good record-keeping.

Safeguarding the Worship Ministry

8. As the worship minister, it is good to make unannounced visits in preschool, children's, or student rehearsals or activities to monitor that these principles are being followed.

9. As the worship minister, you need to be aware of the definition of child abuse in your state. When you observe a situation where you think there is the possibility of child abuse, it must be reported to the police. By not reporting you become part of the situation and could be liable.

10. All adult workers who serve in preschool, children's, or student worship ministry events must be trained to follow these guidelines. A strict adherence to the guidelines protects your children and your worship ministry.

WORSHIP MINISTRY EVENTS AND TRIPS WITH CHILDREN OR STUDENTS

When you plan events or worship ministry trips with children or students, there are a number of principles to consider so that you keep those in your care safe. I am grateful that in my early days of ministry I did not have any major catastrophes. As I think back, I could list a few occurrences that may have turned out much differently except for the grace of the Lord. What are some principles to consider when planning activities away from the church for children or students?

When planning a trip for students such as a mission trip, allow enough budget money to make a pre-trip to the mission location six months in advance. This may not possible for international mission settings but for trips in the states it can make a great impact on your trip planning. During this pre-trip you can set up meetings with those who will guide the mission activities, such as a local pastor, missionary, or association director. You will have the opportunity to visit the actual mission sites and places the group will stay. All of this information is crucial in formulating the logistics of the main trip. Often after a pre-trip to the mission site you may decide to change some of the initial plans in order to be more effective at the mission site. Sometimes you may find that housing or transportation decisions need to be changed. I remember visiting a motel where we had reservations to stay on our mission trip. I immediately noticed that the location did not

Section IV: Discipling through Worship Ministry

appear to be safe because there was a bar adjacent to the motel lobby. As a result of the pre-trip visit we made other arrangements for housing.

An important part of planning a trip away from the church is that you make sure everyone is informed of the plans, activities, and costs. Parents must be kept fully in the information loop when planning events. Information pages with full disclosure on the activity should be put into the hands of the parents. If the event is a mission trip or camp an early meeting with parents is needed. On the night of a parent meeting you should secure medical information and emergency contact numbers for each student. Have a notary of the public present to notarize permission slips of each student. The notarized signature acknowledges that the parents are aware of the details of the trip and give permission for their students to attend.

When something goes wrong on a trip, parents can be upset when the incident occurs during an activity that was not on the itinerary. If you are taking a fun day at the end of the mission trip and going rafting, make sure the parents are aware of the activity. It is the unannounced activities where an occurrence happens that can cause a church to be sued.

Adequate numbers of approved chaperones are needed for trips. Just as you would screen workers for a children's activity at the church, these chaperones all need to be screened and approved to serve as chaperones. Activities that are more risky require more chaperones, such as mission activities in difficult areas of a town. The two-adult rule still applies on trips and careful planning to make sure this takes place is important.

When considering room arrangements for overnight or week-long accommodations, remember that adult chaperones are not to stay in the same rooms as the students. This is sometimes problematic because supervision is necessary; however, it is safer in the long run for students to be housed with students and chaperones with chaperones. If you are reserving a hotel space, look for hotels that have inside hallways. Some older hotels have rooms that open up to the parking lot. This type of hotel is not as safe for your students. If you are utilizing host homes at a church you are visiting, make it clear that no less than two students will stay in a home. Some churches have a policy of not using host homes for their student trips due to abuse issues that have occurred.

As you plan your mission trip or other worship ministry activity, consider the worst-case scenario. What would you do in case of an accident of some sort? If you are driving church vans and there is an accident, what would you do? How would you protect the students? If a student needs emergency treatment, where would you go? Do you have the student's medical form, emergency contact information, and notarized parental form at hand?

I recall a mission trip I was leading a number of years ago where we had a rear tire blowout on a church van while traveling on an interstate highway. There were a total of three church vans in transit and all were in close proximity of each other as we traveled. The van with the tire blowout safely pulled over to the side of the interstate. The students in that van moved a good distance from the highway as we determined the extent of the damage. Then one of the other vans dropped off their students at a fast-food restaurant nearby and came to pick up the stranded students from alongside the road. It was soon determined that the disabled van had some additional damage from the tire blowout and was not travel-worthy. We were about two hours from home. After some phone calls we were able to locate two of our deacons who found another van for us to drive. They delivered the van to us and took the damaged van back for repair. This incident delayed us about six hours. We missed an evening concert the group was planning to share, but everyone was safe and the trip continued.

There were times when we needed to find walk-in clinics for students with medical issues. We made emergency room trips in the middle of the night for other student problems. Students often have allergic reactions to things, sprained ankles, or the need to be stitched up for a cut. How you handle all of these unplanned events is very important. Planning ahead for possible mishaps helps you make good decisions in the moment when they happen. I have a habit of immediately calling parents when something is happening with their child. Hospital workers usually want to speak to a parent concerning treatment options.

Consider the needs of the different age groups as you plan activities or trips. There are some events that are only wise for high school students to do. I recall a canoeing trip for middle school and high school students. We were in a national forest in central Florida going down a spring-fed river that was about four feet deep and eight feet wide. It was a pristine environment in the middle of the forest with no civilization for several miles. My first clue that the middle school students were not suited for the trip came in the first ten minutes of the canoe run when they kept turning over their canoes. Balance was an issue for this age group. A little later down the river we came upon a bank where a fair-sized alligator was resting. Nothing happened, much to my relief, but I quickly decided that perhaps middle school

Section IV: Discipling through Worship Ministry

students would be better suited for a water park activity than a canoe run in a national forest.

Sometimes an activity could be more physically demanding for younger students than for older students. Hiking up a Colorado mountain works well for some older students who may have the muscle development and stamina to push through some steep areas but for a younger student a round of miniature golf may be better suited. When doing these recreational activities consider what you would do if an accident happened. Have you considered the physical needs of your students on an activity, such as the need for water and food? Have you thought about the amount of sun or heat exposure that your students may experience?

Early on I determined that swimming activities for a large group were more than I could handle. Once I took fifty children swimming at a beach. I did have a number of chaperones present but the whole time I was fully aware of how quickly a child could disappear in the water. I decided that an afternoon of water activities on the lawn of the church was just as fun for the children and much less risky of an activity.

An indicator of the risk you may be assuming at an activity can be determined by checking your church's insurance policy. If the insurance company for your church considers the event risky, then you should also. If you are not sure of the insurance company's stance on a particular activity, call them and have them look at your church policy. It could be you would need to purchase some additional insurance from your church insurer for the activity you are planning. Another way to determine the safety of an activity is to take the "my kid" test. Ask yourself the question, "Would I allow my kid to do this activity?"

When traveling with a group of students and making stops at rest areas or restaurants, always keep an eye on what is happening with the students. Assign chaperones to keep watch over the students at stops to make sure the students are safe. Be sure all students are back on the vans or bus before getting back on the road. When you allow students to change seating arrangements to other vans or buses, you might leave a student behind at a rest stop through the confusion.

I believed in "no child left behind" long before the Department of Education came up with this idea. In my first full-time church, we planned an all-night student event that included bowling, skating, miniature golf, and other games. Several church youth groups came together for the event so there were over a hundred students present all night. Our last activity was to travel to a nearby beach and give a devotional as the sun was rising. Obviously, all were quite tired by this point. This beach had a boardwalk with a pavilion. Most of the students sat on benches at the pavilion as we gave the devotion. When it was over the students packed in the church vans and headed back to church so that their parents could pick them up. As we arrived at the church the students dispersed. At that point we quickly learned from a frantic mom that one of our middle school boys was missing. After looking around the church we decided to go back to the beach pavilion, which was ten minutes from the church. Needless to say, I was quite anxious thinking we had lost a kid. Our fears were relieved when we saw him asleep on a bench at the beach pavilion. He fell asleep during the devotion and did not even know he was left behind. This story ended well but it could easily have been a different outcome. I was so grateful that the boy was safe. How easy it is for us to make a mistake that can be life-changing when we are working with children and students. We cannot control every outcome but we can be diligent to plan well to prevent unwanted events.

Worship ministry to children and students requires the leaders to be relentless in protecting these precious gifts from the Lord. We assume a great responsibility when we agree to lead worship ministry events to these age groups. It can be very rewarding if we care enough to put protective principles in place that will keep our children and students safe.

WORSHIP MINISTRY AND ADULTS

How you as a worship minister conduct yourself around other adults is extremely important. When we think about working with children and insuring that there are always two adults available when working with a group of children, the same principle applies when working with adults. I am going to address men in this section but what I say can easily apply to women in ministry.

As a worship minister, you should never be alone with a woman who is not your wife. This applies to times at church or any other place. As men we are so prone to temptation. The time you think you are least likely to be tempted will be the time you fall. How often I have heard of a worship minister having an affair with a woman on his worship team. This kind of temptation develops over a period of time when the minister and lay person let their guards down.

Section IV: Discipling through Worship Ministry

Worship ministers must consider these principles in order to protect their ministries.

1. Worship ministers must ensure that they will not be alone with a woman before or after a rehearsal or service. If you plan to stay late after a rehearsal, ask your wife or another male team member to stay behind with you.

2. Worship ministers must not touch a woman in an inappropriate way. Do not ever send a wrong message in your attempt to show concern or comfort.

3. Worship ministers must be careful in correspondence with women by mail, email, or text message not to send a message that could be misconstrued as a suggestive statement.

4. Worship ministers must not be alone in a car with a woman other than their wife.

5. Worship ministers must not give marital or relationship counseling to a woman unless the woman's husband is present in the room. Single women should be counseled by other women or by a husband-and-wife team.

6. Worship ministers must not be alone with a child or teenage boy or girl.

7. Worship ministers must not visit in the home of a woman. Take your wife with you on the visit.

8. Worship ministers must flee any situation that does not appear to be above reproach.

These principles will protect your family and your ministry. When a minister falls there is a great destruction for the minister's family and his church. We must be wise in our relationships and remember that there is spiritual warfare all around us. 1 Peter 5:8 tells us to "Be sober-minded; be watchful. Your adversary the devil prowls around like a roaring lion, seeking someone to devour." Ministers live their lives with a target on their backs. Do not put yourself in a compromising situation. Every day we must put on the "whole armor of God," as Ephesians 6 reminds us, so that we can withstand the fiery darts of the evil one.

Safeguarding the Worship Ministry

How are you safeguarding your worship ministry? Are you putting into practice good principles as you disciple your children, students, and adults?

CHAPTER 27

When It Is Time to Move

A PASTOR FRIEND OF mine went to a church plant in 1980 right after he finished seminary. After thirty-seven years he is still the pastor of that church. It is now a large church with many active ministries. He is the only senior pastor this church has known. I am sure in his many days of ministry at this church there may have been days when he prayed that the Lord would move him to a new place of ministry because times were difficult. He persevered and will probably retire in a few years having only served this one church since seminary. This is not every minister's story because the Lord does call ministers to new places of ministry. A long tenure at one church is desirable but what if the Lord calls you to a new place of ministry? How can one know when it is time to move to a new place of ministry?

Sometimes we desperately want to move away from a church when times are challenging even though we have no where to go. It is unusual that the Lord would call us away from a place of ministry with no clear direction on a new place of service. In my experience God did not open a door to move when things were going rough. Opportunities to move to a new place of service usually happened when I was content in the ministry work at my church. Unless the Lord is obviously moving you to a new place of ministry, it is best to stay where he has planted you.

To be honest, most places of ministry are difficult. Even in churches where everything seems to be going well there are some challenging aspects to the ministry. The grass is not always greener on the other side. Years ago I would regularly meet with a friend who was a worship minister in a large church. I was serving in a smaller church and was enamored with all that my friend had at his disposal in his church setting. He had a beautiful worship ministry suite with a large music rehearsal area, great equipment, and a staff of worship assistants. As we became more acquainted over time, I discovered that his place of ministry was complicated and at times very difficult. The outward appearance was attractive but behind the scenes all was not as it seemed. We can desire a perfect place of ministry but we will never find this place until we worship with the saints in heaven.

Because I believe the Lord calls us to our places of ministry, I want to be discerning when I consider a new place of ministry. As I look back on the churches I have served, there were times in every place that I had a desire to move to a new place of ministry. This was usually due to a difficulty with the pastor or staff, or some other situation in that place of ministry. Sometimes these feelings would go away after a time and I would find myself more content in my work. There are seasons in our ministries that are easier than others. Determining whether your desire to move is caused by a difficult season or the Lord doing a work in your heart is a matter of serious prayer and meditating on the Word.

I served in a church where there was a great deal of turmoil and conflict among the staff. I was not a part of this conflict and chose to steer clear of taking sides. It was during this time that I earnestly prayed that the Lord would move me to a new place ministry. There were no open doors to move forward. I considered for some time going back to school to work on a doctorate so I could teach. I decided to pursue doctoral work at a large state university in Florida and proceeded to work through all of the initial hurdles to getting accepted into the program. When the time came, I was not invited into the program that year. The school did offer for me to move there, take classes, and resubmit my application the following year. I decided that the Lord was not in this and pressed forward in the current ministry setting despite the turmoil. Not long after being turned down for doctoral studies I ran into a worship minister friend (the one at the large church I mentioned earlier). He said that one of his close pastor friends was looking for a worship pastor and my friend wanted to submit my résumé. After some prayer and discussion with my wife I decided to send my résumé.

Things began happening at a quick pace and soon my wife and I were visiting the church on a weekend in view of a call. We arrived on Friday morning and had meetings Friday night and all day Saturday. They expected me to lead worship Sunday morning, followed by a church vote the next week. By Saturday night I told my wife that I did not believe I was

Section IV: Discipling through Worship Ministry

supposed to move to this church. This was a surprise to her since she knew of my dissatisfaction at my present church setting. She advised me to get some rest, get through the Sunday services, and then see how I felt about this new church after Sunday. In a few days I determined that my desire to stay at my current church was related to a fear of change and the unknown that comes with a new place of service. Even though I was unhappy in the current church, fear of starting over was enough to keep me from moving forward. The church did call us and we accepted. This church became such a wonderful place of ministry.

Toward the end of my eleven years of ministry in this church I became restless in my work. It was hard to decide what was causing the restlessness. I think some of it was the weekly schedule of a growing church with three Sunday morning worship services and a Sunday night service each week. I was tired. I also thought that I had done all I knew to do at this church in the area of worship ministry. At my last church I was dissatisfied with the conflict and turmoil of the church staff but at this current church the restlessness was in me. For some time I prayed about going back to school for doctoral work despite that fact that I could not see how I could make this work financially with the needs of my family. There were days I would determine that I was crazy to think about leaving a wonderful place of ministry and that the school idea was not reasonable. I was also forty-one years old.

After visiting Southern Baptist Seminary for the third time, I determined that the Lord was leading me to study at this place. I was not yet ready to take the leap of faith to make this happen. On my last visit to the school we discovered that a nearby church was looking for a worship pastor and that they were willing for me to pursue doctoral studies as I served the church. They also provided a home. The Lord was opening doors and helping me to see that he was quite capable of handling the details of this move. Within a month we resigned from my current church, moved to Kentucky, began doctoral work, and started serving in the new church. Some may say I was having a midlife crisis but looking back I believe the Lord was in my restlessness. He was using this restlessness to move me on to a new challenge.

I have the gift of years at this point to look back and see the Lord's hand in the places where I have served in worship ministry. Here are some considerations on determining when it's time to move to a new place of ministry.

When It Is Time to Move

1. Every time things get difficult in your current ministry it does not mean it is a sign to move. There are going to be days (and possibly seasons) in every ministry setting when times are tough.

2. Spending time in prayer and meditation in the Word is important at all times, especially when you are trying to discern the Lord's will in your ministry.

3. Seeking wise counsel from older trusted ministers can help you determine if this desire to move is of the Lord or just an attempt to escape a difficult ministry season.

4. Do not take things into your own hands. If the Lord has not opened a new place of service for you, stay where you are until he does.

5. When you hear of an opportunity, remember that every open door does not necessarily reflect the Lord's leadership.

6. If you are trying to make a decision when you are tired or possibly dealing with depression, realize that you are probably not in the best state of mind to think clearly.

7. Sometimes the Lord will open a door for a new place of ministry when you least expect it. He may even change the whole direction of your ministry, such as he did when I went back to school.

8. When all is said and done, it will be a step of faith for you to launch out into a new ministry. The Lord may open the door for you but you will have to step through the door. Sometimes the most difficult part of the change is to go from the known to the unknown.

9. It could happen that you may be asked to leave a church. This could be related to a new pastor coming who wants to make some changes. It could be from no fault of your own. When this happens remember that God is sovereign. This does not come as a surprise to him. He is in the midst of all of the details and working in ways you do not even know. Reach out to mentors in your life and ministry friends who can pray with you and offer wise counsel. The Lord will use this difficult time in your life to shape you and prepare you for the next place of ministry. When you leave a difficult place of ministry do not burn bridges. Do not lash out at leadership in your resignation letter or say negative things to lay people about the church. Be gracious and kind even when you are hurt.

Section IV: Discipling through Worship Ministry

10. Let me encourage you to let God orchestrate the changes in your ministry. It is tempting to get ahead of God and attempt to make things happen more quickly. We must wait on him.

What a privilege it is to be called to a place of ministry. Working with the men, women, and children in worship ministry is rewarding despite the fact that times may be difficult. As you serve, plan to stay for the long haul. Desire to be at your place of ministry for many years so you can see all that the Lord will do among his people. When you go to a place of ministry, do not view it as a stepping stone to a better place of ministry later. See this place of ministry as a place you will serve until he moves you to another church or on to glory.

CHAPTER 28

Some Closing Thoughts

WORSHIP MINISTRY, LIKE OTHER ministry positions, is a blessing and a challenge. Seeing persons come to Christ and grow in their faith is unquestionably gratifying. It is also a difficult place due to the sinfulness of those in the church (including yourself and the leadership). Helping people work through life's challenges can leave the minister frustrated and worn. As I look back I am grateful to the Lord for the opportunity to serve in the local church. At the end of this guidebook for worship ministry, here are some closing challenges to the worship minister.

PRACTICE THE SPIRITUAL DISCIPLINES

Your ministry will rise or fall on your commitment to the spiritual disciplines: prayer, Bible Study, quiet time, meditation, Scripture memory, and journaling. You minister out of the overflow of your life in Christ.

SEEK PURITY

"Our salvation and the salvation of those who hear us week after week depend in large measure on our faithful attention to personal holiness and sound teaching."[1] The most important thing your people need from you is your personal holiness. Run from temptation and fix your eyes on Jesus (Heb 12:1–2). Remove stumbling blocks that cause you to sin. You are

---

1. Piper, *Brothers, We Are Not Professionals*, 106.

either moving forward in your fight for holiness or you are drifting. We do not stand still in this struggle. "Keep watch on yourself, lest you too be tempted" (Gal 6:1). If you believe that you cannot be tempted in a certain area, you are setting yourself up for a fall. Guard your heart. Do not let your musical talent get ahead of your character. Live above reproach.

LOVE YOUR FAMILY

Your first place of service is to your family. Love your spouse. Love your children. Give them priority in your schedule. If you lose your family, you lose your ministry.

SERVE YOUR PASTOR, THE CHIEF UNDER-SHEPHERD

Your pastor is the chief worship leader. He has been charged with the responsibility to oversee the local body of Christ—the church. Serve your pastor. Communicate with your pastor all things, positive and negative. Never talk negatively about your pastor to lay people or church staff. Do not let your pastor be surprised.

REJECT PASSIVITY

Ministers must be outgoing in their work at the church and outside the church. Musicians have a tendency to be introverted. You must learn to initiate eye contact and greet people. Lead your people. Work through conflicts. Do not be moody. Ask the Lord to help you be bold.

BE A GOOD ADMINISTRATOR

Musicians can be undisciplined in time management and work ethic. Be a good steward of your time and work. You do not get a "pass" if you are weak in this area. No matter how musically gifted you are, if you do not do well in administering the worship ministry, you will not be at your church very long before you are asked to leave.

Some Closing Thoughts

COMMUNICATE, COMMUNICATE, COMMUNICATE

Your ministry will sink or swim on your communication skills. You must communicate with your pastor, your staff, your worship teams, and your congregation. This requires advanced planning and constant two-way communication.

MINISTER TO PEOPLE

Music is not your focus. You were called to work with people and care for their souls. Don't view people as commodities for your worship ministry. How well are you discipling the people in your charge?

SERVE THE GENERATIONS

Reach all ages at your church through worship ministry. Edify and equip. Work yourself out of a job by training people to do what you do. Raise up worship leaders among the next generation: singers, guitar players, pianists, drummers, string players, and horn players. When the Lord calls you away from your place of service, leave the worship ministry much stronger than when you arrived.

MODEL SERVANT LEADERSHIP

Jesus is our model when seeking to lead others. Serve your worship team and congregation with great humility. Never ask someone to do something you are not willing to do yourself.

FIGHT SPIRITUAL BATTLES WITH SPIRITUAL WEAPONS

When conflict or difficult situations occur in your ministry, remember to apply spiritual tools and weapons (Eph 6:1–20). There is spiritual warfare taking place for the souls of your people and for the existence of the church. Bathe your ministry in prayer.

Section IV: Discipling through Worship Ministry

REMEMBER THE CHURCH BELONGS TO CHRIST

The church where you serve is not your church. Christ died for the church and the church belongs to him. Christ has given you a stewardship to love and serve his church. Never forget you are serving Christ when you are serving your church. Do your work as unto Christ. You have an awesome stewardship and responsibility. Cherish the opportunity the Lord has given you to do this.

Bibliography

Bradley, Randall. *From Postlude to Prelude: Music Ministry's Other Six Days.* St Louis: Morningstar, 2004.
Bridges, Jerry. *The Pursuit of Holiness.* Colorado Springs: NavPress, 2006.
Chapell, Bryan. *Christ-Centered Worship.* Grand Rapids: Baker, 2009.
Crabtree, Jack. *Better Safe than Sued: Keeping Out of Trouble in Youth Ministry.* El Cajon, CA: Youth Specialties, 2009.
Dale, R.W. *Nine Lectures on Preaching: Delivered at Yale.* London: Hodder and Stoughton, 1877. https://archive.org/details/ninelecturesonpr00daleiala.
DeYoung, Kevin. "Reaching the Next Generation, Hold Them with Holiness." October 21, 2009. https://blogs.thegospelcoalition.org/kevindeyoung/2009/10/21/reaching-the-next-generation-hold-them-with-holiness/.
Hustad, Donald P. *Jubilate II: Church Music in Worship and Renewal.* Chicago: Hope, 1993.
Kauflin, Bob. *Worship Matters: Leading Others to Encounter the Greatness of God.* Wheaton: Crossway, 2008.
Kinnaman, David. *You Lost Me: Why Young Christians Are Leaving the Church and Rethinking Faith.* Grand Rapids: Baker, 2011.
Liesch, Barry. *The New Worship: Straight Talk on Music and the Church.* Grand Rapids: Baker, 2001.
Marshall, Collin, and Tony Payne. *The Trellis and the Vine: The Ministry Mind-Shift that Changes Everything.* Sydney, Australia: Matthias Media, 2009.
Menconi, Peter. *The Intergenerational Church: Understanding Congregations from WWII to www.com.* Littleton, CO: Mt. Sage, 2008.
Mohler, Albert R., et al. *The Call to Ministry.* Louisville: SBTS, 2013.
National Association of Schools of Music (NASM). "Health Document." https://nasm.arts-accredit.org/publications/brochures-advisories/nasm-pama-hearing-health/.
Noland, Rory. *The Heart of the Artist: A Character-Building Guide for You and Your Ministry Team.* Grand Rapids: Zondervan, 1999.
Piper, John. *Brothers, We Are Not Professionals: A Plea to Pastors for Radical Ministry.* Nashville: Broadman and Holman, 2002.
Piper, John. "Singing and Making Melody to the Lord." December 28, 1997. http://www.desiringgod.org/messages/singing-and-making-melody-to-the-lord.
Rosenthal, Shane. "An Interview with J. I. Packer: The State of Evangelicalism." In *Reformed Worship* (2008) 40–44.

Bibliography

Sanders, J. Oswald. *Spiritual Leadership: Principles of Excellence for Every Believer.* Chicago: Moody, 1994.

Spurgeon, Charles H. *Lectures to My Students.* Peabody, MA: Hendrickson, 2010.

Stott, John R. W. *The Preacher's Portrait: Some New Testament Word Studies.* Grand Rapids: Eerdmans, 1961.

Taylor, Howard. *Hudson Taylor's Spiritual Secrets.* Chicago: Moody, 2009.

Thompson, Bard. *Liturgies of the Western Church.* Philadelphia: Fortress, 1980.

Webber, Robert E. *Ancient-Future Faith: Rethinking Evangelicalism for a Postmodern World.* Grand Rapids: Baker, 1999.

www.ingramcontent.com/pod-product-compliance
Lightning Source LLC
Chambersburg PA
CBHW050811160426
43192CB00010B/1717